MAKE MONEY ON THE STOCK EXCHANGE

by Robert Leach, ACCA

GW00727949

W. FOULSHAM & CO. LTD.

London ● New York ● Toronto ● Cape Town ● Sydney

W. Foulsham & Company Limited
Yeovil Road, Slough, Berkshire, SL1 4JH

ISBN 0-572-01447-3

Printed in Great Britain at
St Edmundsbury Press, Bury St Edmunds.

Contents

7. Choosing Your Shares   41

1. Preliminaries – 2. Choosing the shares – 3. Methods of choosing – 4. Ethical investment – 5. 'Sid's' shares – 6. Sources of information

8. When to Buy and Sell   48

1. General considerations – 2. Advice – 3. Track record – 4. Analysis of share prices – 5. Moving averages – 6. Charting – 7. Computer programs

9. Keeping a Record   60

1. Introduction – 2. Financial accounts – 3. Management accounts – 4. Recording moving averages – 5. Refinements to the system: longer averages – 6. Improving the system: including general measures

10. Tax   66

1. Introduction – 2. Stamp duty – 3. Value added tax – 4. Income tax – 5. Capital gains tax – 6. Inheritance tax

11. Personal Equity Plans   71

1. What are Personal Equity Plans? – 2. The rules

12. Quick Guide to Company Law   73

1. Limited liability – 2. Types of share – 3. Par value – 4. Types of share issue – 5. Stages in issuing shares – 6. Transfer and registration – 7. Shareholders' rights – 8. Shareholders' perks – 9. Takeovers

13. Other Types of Investment   85

1. Unit trusts – 2. Gilts – 3. Traded options – 4. Other markets – 5. Overseas shares – 6. Property – 7. Venture capital

1. Why Invest on the Stock Exchange?

1. Introduction

The Stock Exchange provides the opportunity for you to invest your money directly in the industrial base of the economy. By buying a company's shares, you actually own part of that company. The shareholders collectively own the whole company, and, ultimately, are entitled to all its net profits.

The investor is effectively lending money to a company for it to fund its trading. In return for lending the company your money, the company gives part of its profit to you. The Stock Exchange allows you to sell the shares when you want, thus making it worthwhile to buy shares which, in turn, allows companies to raise the finance they need.

Even if the companies you pick only perform in line with the economy generally, you can reasonably expect your income from the investment to be at least twice what you would have obtained by putting the money in a bank or building society.

The reason for this is that the banks and building societies also obtain their funds to pay their depositors by investing in companies. From the profits they receive they must deduct all their own expenses and overheads and keep some money aside for a rainy day. By investing directly in the companies you cut out that middle stage.

This does not mean that you should never deposit money in a bank or building society, as there are other advantages which the small investor must consider.

The income from shares is derived from two sources:

    i dividends
    ii profit on sale.

Section 3 'Capital and profit' explains more about this.

Apart from shares there is an amazing array of other investments. Some, like unit trusts, are effectively a halfway house between share ownership and deposit account. Others, like traded options, are much riskier than share ownership.

2. Cautions

Before putting your life savings into shares, there are some fundamental points that need to be considered:

i Share prices can fall as well as rise (as many investors discovered in October 1987). Although most companies' shares do appreciate in value, there is no guarantee that any *particular* company's shares will rise. If the company goes bust, your shares are worth nothing. Even if the company survives, your shares may be worth much less than you paid for them. The higher return generally on shares over, say, a building society deposit, normally compensates for this extra *risk*. Chapter 8 explains how to minimise and offset this risk.

ii You may not be able to get your money back when you want it. You should never invest in shares any money that you need for a specific purpose, e.g. moving house, a holiday, a daughter's wedding, etc. Your profits from investment depend on being able to sell the shares at the right time. If you are forced to sell them at another time you will receive less for them. It is always advisable to have money for special events or emergencies readily available in the bank or building society.

iii It involves your time. In order to maximise your profits generally you should keep an eye on both the economy (and other relevant matters) in general and on what your companies and their shares are doing in particular. You may also be involved in charting or plotting share prices. You will have additional accounting and tax requirements.

iv Commission can wipe out the profit on a small deal. When you buy and sell shares you can become liable to pay commission (plus VAT), and stamp duty. These charges can easily wipe out the profit you would otherwise have made. As a rough guide, it is usually inadvisable to hold less than £500 worth of shares in any one company.

v Real profit may be less than paper profit. It is easy to boast that shares bought for £500 are now worth £800 according to today's *Financial Times*, but that ignores the simple fact that *you cannot sell your shares for the price quoted in the newspaper*. The prices quoted are an average of the buying and selling prices. You will sell them for less than that figure, and be liable for commission and (possibly) tax. The prices quoted are always historic. There will often be some movement between reading the price and selling the share.

3. Capital and Profit

Your income from shares is derived from dividends and (hopefully) the profit when you sell them.

Dividends are usually paid twice a year, though there is nothing to stop a company paying them more or less frequently. If the company is having a hard time it will not pay a dividend at all. (Sheffield Wednesday Football Club last paid a dividend in 1935.)

One dividend is paid soon after the annual accounts have been published and is known as the *final dividend*. The other is paid six months earlier and is known as the *interim dividend*.

In deciding which shares to buy, you will need to consider (among other things) your need for *capital growth* and your need for *regular income*. This will largely affect your policy towards the shares, rather than which shares you buy, because, as a general rule, a company that has a good dividend record (and thus provides regular income) will see its shares increase in value as a result. Thus the companies that provide a good regular dividend will tend to be the same companies that can make you a large profit on selling their shares.

If you sell shares in such a company you are effectively selling your right to participate in that company's future prosperity. If, after you have sold the shares, the company ceases to be prosperous and returns bad results, your decision will have been wise indeed.

As a rough yardstick, dividends provide a yield of about 5 per cent of your investment, but the dividends grow at about

10 per cent a year. This means that it is still worthwhile holding shares just for the dividends, but only if you intend holding them for some years.

The table shows how such a dividend compares with a deposit account paying 8 per cent interest per annum on an investment of £1000.

Comparison of deposit account and investment

	Deposit account		Shares	
	Interest	Cumulative	Dividend	Cumulative
Year 1	£80	£80	£50	£50.00
Year 2	£80	£160	£55	£105.00
Year 3	£80	£240	£60.50	£165.50
Year 4	£80	£320	£66.55	£232.05
Year 5	£80	£400	£73.20	£305.25
Year 6	£80	£480	£80.52	£385.77
Year 7	£80	£560	£88.57	£474.34
Year 8	£80	£640	£97.43	£571.77
Year 9	£80	£720	£107.17	£678.94
Year 10	£80	£800	£117.89	£796.83
Year 11	£80	£880	£129.68	£926.51
Year 12	£80	£960	£142.65	£1069.16

You will see that, using typical figures, it takes six years for the dividend to reach the same figure as the deposit account interest, and ten years for the cumulative dividend income to reach the cumulative interest.

However the *capital sum* you can withdraw from the deposit account is still only £1000. The capital value of your shares is likely to have (at the very least) doubled in the period.

You may notice that the table ignores inflation. The effect of inflation is that the £960 is not directly comparable with the £1069.16, as some of the former will have been earned earlier when the pounds were worth more. This, however, has little effect on the overall results, as the rate of inflation is effectively reflected in the dividends and share values anyway.

4. Getting Started

There are four ways in which to start:

  i unit trusts
 ii new issues
iii dry run portfolios,
 iv Personal Equity Plans (Chapter 12).

A unit trust is an investment vehicle which buys and sells shares. You buy units in the trust (which are the equivalent of shares in it). Those units rise and fall according to how well the whole fund is managed. The advantage is that you are effectively in a spread of companies far wider than you could sensibly manage otherwise, so your risk is minimised. Some unit trusts *do* lose value, but never right down to zero as a share can.

In 1986, the year of the 'Big Bang', £100 invested in the best performing unit trust (Legal and General Far East) was worth £227.40 at the end of the year. £100 invested in the worst performing unit trust (MIM Britannia Universal Energy) was worth £81.80. The extremes of unit trusts were thus +127.4 per cent and –18.2 per cent, compared with +831 per cent and –77 per cent for shares (see section 5).

New issues are a sensible start for a novice investor as there are no commission fees, making the purchase more cost-effective, and there is usually plenty of press coverage, enabling you to understand the nature of the company's business.

The Conservative Government's privatisation plans have also been remarkably successful. Out of all the companies privatised, only Britoil and BP shares have failed to go to an immediate premium, but even there your loss would have been small. No other country has attempted flotations on the scale of British Gas or the Trustee Savings Bank and the world has watched with interest.

Often new issues are for partly-paid shares. This is explained more fully in Chapter 12, but, put simply, it means that initially you pay for only part of your shareholdings and will have to pay the rest later. The prospectus or advertisement from which you apply for your shares will tell you when.

Dry run portfolios are when you invent a portfolio without actually buying the shares. You manage this fictitious portfolio (Chapter 2 tells you how) and decide when to sell your shares and what to buy instead.

This exercise gives you experience of investment management without risking any money. When you feel confident enough, you can start to use real money.

It is important though that you do not cheat! Because the shares you 'bought' last week have fallen by 10 per cent, don't pretend that you didn't buy them. And remember to allow for commissions, stamp duty, etc.

5. Size of the Risk

It is rare for a public company to go bust these days. The worst that usually happens is that its share price plummets because the Stock Exchange loses faith in it (usually because it has lost faith in its management).

In 1986 the worst performing company was Pict Petroleum which lost 77 per cent of its value. Among larger companies (over £10m) the worst was Oceonics which lost 68 per cent.

However the gains are much greater. The best performing company in 1986 was Owen and Robinson (jewellers) which gained 831 per cent. James Ferguson (textiles) was second with an increase of 675 per cent. In larger companies, Nu-Swift Industries performed best with an increase of 269 per cent. These figures are taken for the whole calendar year. By deciding *when* to buy and sell (see Chapter 8), even greater returns can be achieved.

6. Consumer Capitalism

Private investment is actively encouraged by the Conservative Government under its policy of 'consumer capitalism' – encouraging us all to own shares.

In his 1987 Budget statement, the Chancellor of the Exchequer announced that there were now 8.5m individual shareholders. This is about 20 per cent of the entire adult population and three times as many as there were in 1979. British Gas alone is estimated to have created 2.21m.

By the end of 1986 1.25m employees were participating in profit-sharing and SAYE schemes. Millions more were participating indirectly through unit trusts and pension schemes.

Some nationalised industries have been 'privatised'. The

1986 flotations of British Gas and TSB were the largest the world has ever seen. All these (with the exceptions of Britoil and BP) have been extremely successful, not only raising billions for the Government but forcing these companies to operate more efficiently by subjecting them to market forces.

Further encouragement to the private investor came with easier and cheaper access to shares as a result of the 'Big Bang' on 27 October 1986. This has cut some commission rates from 1.65 to 1 per cent. When Wall Street (the New York stock exchange) abolished fixed commissions in May 1975, the small investor was initially ignored in the excitement. Then companies realised the attraction of marketing to the small investor, who is now spoilt for choice. There are already signs that London will follow suit.

Another plank in the same policy was the introduction of Personal Equity Plans in the 1986 Budget, which give generous tax incentives to private investors. These are discussed more fully in Chapter 12.

Had a Labour government been elected in 1987, it would have been unlikely to continue this policy, but it is unclear as to how far they would have felt able to reverse it. Plans to renationalise British Telecom had already been dropped, and in the campaign for the June 1987 General Election the term 'nationalisation' was replaced by the less odious-sounding 'social ownership'. Bryan Gould MP even suggested, at the 1987 Labour Party conference, that some types of share ownership could usefully be used as part of Labour policy.

It should be remembered, though, that consumer capitalism is not just a UK phenomenon. It was a socialist government which privatised the French prison service. Communist China opened its first stock exchange in 1986, and even Soviet Russia has allowed some privatisation.

7. Investor Protection

The investor is protected against unscrupulous practice by many legal and supervisory provisions.

If you lose money as a result of fraud or the financial failure of a member of the London Stock Exchange, your loss will be made up by the Stock Exchange's Compensation Fund. This has ensured that no investor has thus been defrauded of money since 1951.

Other investment companies must be registered with the Securities and Investments Board which has, at the time of writing, put forward draft compensation regulations. The proposal is that the investor who loses money because of a dispute will be covered up to £100,000. If the money is lost because the firm goes bust, he will be covered up to £48,000.

There is, of course, no protection if you make a loss simply by making unwise investments.

8. Golden Rules to Investing

    i Only invest spare capital. Do not use money that is earmarked for a specific purpose or is likely to be needed suddenly. Do not borrow money to invest.

    ii Before using real money, do a dry run using an imaginary portfolio.

    iii When you do start using real money, only commit part of your spare capital, perhaps a third, until you feel more experienced.

    iv Keep to unit trusts and blue chip companies until you feel confident enough to move to more speculative investments. Do not buy traded options until you feel you are an expert.

    v Do not feel proprietorial about your shares. You may get a great kick out of knowing that you own so much of a particular company, but do not let this prevent you selling the shares. Many people have lost money (and the opportunity of making it) by holding on to shares for sentimental reasons. If you cannot help feeling sentimental about your investments, buy a painting instead.

    vi Remember that you have not made a profit until you have the cash in your hands.

    vii Do not grieve over the losses you have made, nor over the missed opportunities. Think positively and enjoy your profits.

    viii Do not let beginner's luck or an initial mishap deter you. However, if it becomes clear that you have no aptitude for such things, stop before it's too late.

2. How to Buy and Sell Shares

1. Who to Use

Shares are normally bought and sold by a stockbroker. There is nothing to stop you finding your own buyer, agreeing a price with him and transacting the paperwork yourself (though the law does stop you doing so for another seller). This however assumes that you can find such a person. The Stock Exchange is much more efficient in doing this on your behalf.

The main banks now also offer private investors a good service. New schemes are launched almost monthly. Further details are given on page 18.

You can also buy and sell your shares through some accountants or solicitors, though this is usually only advisable if you have to use their services for other purposes as well, such as executorship, trust management or tax planning.

There are also a few independent share shops where securities can be bought like oranges at a greengrocer. Debenhams successfully launched a share shop in 1987.

Share shops initially suffered adverse publicity because of City Investment Centres which ran two such shops and was closed down by the DTI early in 1986. Legislation to protect investors who lose money in share shops has been proposed. In the meantime, it is worth checking on the share shops (for example by asking your bank manager) before using one.

If you decide to use a stockbroker, Chapter 4 will help you in making your choice, while stockbrokers and the services they offer are listed in Appendix A.

An exception to this procedure is when you buy a new issue. Here you apply directly to the company on a form provided (either in a prospectus or in a newspaper).

2. Managed or Not

Your shareholdings are collectively known as a 'portfolio'.

In addition to asking a stockbroker to buy and sell shares at your specific request, you can ask him to 'manage' your shares. This is known as a 'discretionary portfolio' and means that *the stockbroker* decides when to buy and sell shares, and what shares to buy.

A halfway house is an 'advisory' service, where the stockbroker gives you the advice but you decide whether to buy or sell.

Stockbrokers sometimes make an extra charge for managing a portfolio but usually require the portfolio to be of a standard size, typically £5000.

How much discretion you allow the stockbroker depends on you. You can require him to notify you before making a transaction; you can limit the amount he can sell; you can set prices above or below which he *must* (or must not) buy or sell. Certain standard forms of instruction are included in the glossary.

In practice such restrictions should be as few as possible. Basically either you should manage your own portfolio or allow your stockbroker to do so.

3. Instructions

Buying and selling shares is one of the few remaining areas where verbal instructions are good enough. Remember that once you have given your instructions to a stockbroker by telephone *you are committed*. The motto of the Stock Exchange is 'My Word is My Bond'.

If you are buying shares, your stockbroker will send you a contract note. This is *not* a share certificate. The contract note shows what shares he has bought, their price, and the commission and other charges for doing so. You should check that the details on it are correct. If you have an account with the stockbroker, the balance will be debited to your account. Otherwise it will be accompanied by a demand for payment by Account Day. Your name is added to the company's register of members (the company law aspect is explained more in Chapter 12) and you will be sent a share certificate.

Payment for shares is not immediate. The Stock Exchange

breaks up the year into two-week periods called 'accounts'. Six days after the end of these accounts is 'Account Day' or 'Settlement Day' when the stockbrokers pay each other for the business they have transacted. You must pay your stockbroker by this day. The date will be shown on your contract note.

If you are selling shares, you instruct your broker accordingly. This will either be to sell 'at best' or only above a certain figure. You then complete and sign a transfer form and send it with the share certificate to the stockbroker. The proceeds are either credited to your account or a cheque is sent to you.

4. Share Certificates

If you have bought shares, you will later receive a share certificate. These used to be works of art and were often hung on the wall as things of aesthetic beauty. The demands of the current age mean that they are now more likely to be computer print-outs.

Share certificates must be kept in a safe place. Although it *is* possible to obtain a replacement certificate, it is a time-consuming (and possibly costly) business. You may not be able to buy or sell shares while the certificate is lost.

Bearer certificates (comparatively rare now) *are* irreplaceable. Unlike ordinary share certificates, they are not evidence of share ownership but actually constitute ownership. Ownership passes simply by handing over the certificate, just like handing over a pound coin.

5. What the Stockbroker Does

The stockbroker, then, seeks to buy or sell what you want at the best price.

Traditionally this used to be done by walking round the floor of the Stock Exchange to the (now) hexagonal booths and haggling with the market-makers (formerly jobbers), writing down the bargains in notebooks. The public could watch the action on the floor from a public gallery.

Nowadays the trading is done almost entirely by computer from offices, with the result that the floor is now almost deserted. It is intended to close the floor completely.

6. The Banks

The four main banks all offer a good share-dealing service to private investors.

Barclays Bank launched Barclayshare on 19 October 1987. By March 1988 it will be available at all the bank's 2,000 main branches. The investor gets a share-dealing service with portfolio management and may elect also to have personal investment advice. The dealing is done either through the branches or by telephone between 8.30am and 5.30pm. Settlement is routed direct to a customer's existing bank account at Barclays, or a special new account, the Barclayshare Investor Account (which pays interest on credit balances). This is done on the day after settlement day, cutting out paperwork delays. The bank charges commission of 1.25 per cent for deals up to £5,000, 0.75 per cent for the next £10,000 and 0.5 per cent thereafter. The minimum commission is £16. The subscription is £10 a half-year for the dealing service, and £15 a quarter for the advisory service.

National Westminster Bank has a computerised dealing facility in 245 of its branches. The facility was launched in 1986 and dealt with only one share issue at a time, in practice always the last big privatisation issue. The facility was abandoned for BP. It is planned to extend the service to most, or all alpha stocks in 1988. The big advantage of this system is that you can walk out with a cheque three and a half minutes after handing in a letter of allotment or share certificate with proof of your identity. A normal share-dealing service exists for other branches and shares. The bank charges commission of 1.5 per cent for deals up to £5,000; and then at reducing rates from 1 to 0.2 per cent. Minimum commission is £20.

The Midland Bank has opened a share shop in its branch at New Street, Birmingham and its brokers have also opened a share shop in a building society branch. These are being watched to see how they should be developed. Otherwise normal share dealing is available at branches. The bank charges 1.5 per cent for deals up to £8,000, and 0.55 per cent above. Minimum commission is £20.

Lloyds Bank has a Teleshare service which offers a real time telephone link with the Stock Exchange. They also have Sharedeal, a dealing service through brokers. The commission is 1.5 per cent with a minimum of £20 and a maximum of £150. To this the bank adds its own charge, to a maximum of £5.

3. How Much Does It Cost?

1. Buying and Selling Prices

Shares are bought at one price and sold at another (lower) price. The price will often vary according to the number of shares bought or sold. The difference is called the 'spread'. When expressed as an amount of money (the dealer's margin), it is called the 'turn'.

Stockbrokers derive their income from two sources:

    i commission and
    ii the 'turn'.

Sometimes the stockbrokers will waive one of these sources.

The price quoted in the newspapers is midway between the two *and is not the price at which you can buy or sell your shares*. First, the price will probably have moved before you can buy or sell anyway. But also you will buy above the quoted price, and sell below it.

The extent of the spread depends on whether the shares are *alpha*, *beta*, *gamma* or *delta* shares (see below). There are no rules governing what the spread will be, but research has shown that it tends to be:

    alpha shares: 0.87 per cent
    beta shares: 1.75 per cent
    gamma shares: 3.1 per cent.

Before the 'Big Bang' the spread on alpha shares was 1.1 per cent.

The less the spread, the less profit you lose on selling them.

2. Alpha, Beta, Gamma and Delta Shares

Since the Big Bang (27 October 1986), quoted shares are divided into alpha, beta, gamma and delta categories.

Alpha shares are the most commonly traded companies. (See Chapter 7, section 2.) Beta shares are other companies that have a full listing. Gamma shares are 'second-line' shares, often quoted on the Unlisted Securities Market. Delta shares are any other shares in which there are at least two market-makers.

3. Commission

Since the Big Bang dealers have been free to charge what commission they like. Many have kept to pre-Big Bang rates which are:

up to £7000	1.65 per cent
from £7000	0.55 per cent.

If the commission has to be split, e.g. with a bank or another broker, it may be a little higher, though rarely will it be more than 1.65 per cent. Fees may also be higher for dealing in foreign shares, where 2 per cent is a typical rate.

Often there is a minimum fee, typically £12 per transaction.

4. Example

We shall assume there is an alpha share which sells for £1.50 and can be bought for £1.48. We wish to trade 500 shares.

Buying			Selling		
500 @ £1.50		£750.00	500 @ £1.48		£740.00
Less: transfer stamp		9.00	*Less*: contract stamp	0.10	
contract stamp		0.10	commission @ 1.65%	12.21	
commission @			VAT @ 15% on		
1.65%		12.38	commission	1.83	
VAT @ 15% on					
commission		1.86			14.14
		£773.34			£725.86

4. How to Choose Your Broker

1. General Considerations

The best recommendation for any broker (as for any trader) is personal recommendation.

In the absence of this, you can rely on other criteria such as:

    i size,
    ii location,
   iii specialities,
   iv charges,
    v service offered, and
   vi general helpfulness.

Although stockbrokers have been allowed to advertise for over twenty years, few of them do, and such advertisements as do appear are often unhelpful.

When you have chosen a broker, you will be allocated to one of their managers. The quality of service you receive will depend more on this man's personal abilities than on those of the firm as a whole.

Any investor with a portfolio up to £5000 is regarded as a small investor. Some stockbrokers would put the figure higher. At this level there is limited scope for shopping around.

Having chosen a stockbroker or brokers from the list in Appendix A, it is advisable to ring up the firm, say you are a new investor and would like to speak someone about using their services, and see what reaction you get.

If you find yourself hanging on to an unanswered telephone, and the person you eventually talk to is unhelpful and a bit shirty, ring someone else. However curt the person may be to you, there really is no point in complaining to anyone about him. Let it pass.

Useful questions to ask are:

  i what are your charges?
  ii can you advise me on suitable investments?
  iii how much do you think I should invest in each type of investment? (This means how much in UK shares, overseas shares, unit trusts, and gilts.)

It is usually advisable to act a bit daft and not let on what you already know about how the markets work. This way you can check on the quality of advice given.

There is no point in asking more questions for the sake of it. If after asking your three questions and playing the dim investor, he is not sounding helpful, try someone else. Remember, though, that time is money to a stockbroker and there is a limit to how much time he can spend talking to you. Ten minutes is a long time. In the United States small investors are often strictly rationed as to the amount of time they can have. When their three minutes (or whatever) is up, the stockbroker just puts the telephone down, even in the middle of a sentence. The UK stockbroker is usually more polite, but that will quickly change if small investors insist on using up stockbrokers' time.

Once you have found your stockbroker, stay with him unless there are compelling reasons to move. Loyalty usually pays off.

2. Size and Location

Size can be a useful criterion, on the basis that a firm will only grow to a large size if it has consistently offered a good service to its clients. Also, a large firm will have better research facilities and other resources.

This must be weighed against the fact that a large firm may concentrate on big business from pension funds and insurance companies, and not be interested in the 'Sids' of this world.

The largest stockbroking firm is (and has been for many years) James Capel & Co. But the firm with the largest private client department is Grieveson Grant, now part of Kleinwort Grieveson.

The top twenty (as published by City Research Associates) are given below.

1 James Capel & Co.
2 Hoare Govett
3 Rowe and Pitman
4 Scrimgeour Vickers
5 Phillips and Drew
6 Wood Mackenzie
7 Grieveson Grant (now Kleinwort Grieveson)
8 Cazenove
9 W. Greenwell
10 Barclays de Zoete Wedd
11 Laing and Cruickshank
12 County Securities
13 Messel & Co.
14 Vickers da Costa
15 Simon and Coates
16 Quilter Goodison & Co.
17 Buckmaster and Moore
18 Laurie Millbank
19 Grenfell and Colgrave
20 Capel-Cure Myers.

Location is a less important factor as most business is done by telephone. There are, however, a few advantages in using a firm near to you: it makes it easy to visit them, for example.

A list of stockbroking firms, with addresses, details of services offered and commission rates, is given in Appendix A.

5. What Affects Share Prices?

1. General Considerations

Large doctoral theses have been written on what affects share prices.

At its simplest prices are affected by two sets of factors:

   i those which affect the economy as a whole,
   ii those which affect just the company or its line of business.

These are known respectively as the alpha coefficient and the beta factor. (These terms have nothing to do with alpha and beta shares.)

The alpha coefficient is, to some extent, measured by the Financial Times indices.

But there are many factors that affect the economy and there is no substitute for keeping up to date by reading a good newspaper. (Television is not an alternative.)

2. Political Influence

The economy is affected by many considerations. Probably the most significant is the political state of the country.

The Stock Exchange prefers a Conservative government to a Labour one, and therefore something which is good for the Conservative party (a good conference, good showing in the polls or a by-election, etc.) will help share prices.

Remember that markets reflect events *before* they happen, in other words the market-makers anticipate the most likely outcome. Early in 1987, for instance, the markets decided that the Conservative party had already won the next election and thus the markets were correspondingly bullish. If they had got it completely wrong you would have seen a large fall in share prices the day after Labour won the election instead.

On this basis the Stock Exchange has correctly predicted the results of the last eight UK general elections (which is more than the opinion polls have done), with the result that there have been no marked fluctuations during general election periods. However, during these times the markets are prone to react more markedly than usual (this is called a 'nervous' market).

Part of the Stock Market's secret is that where the result of an election is unclear, or if a hung parliament is possible, investors can shift away from shares affected by political considerations to overseas equities and gilts.

Political factors other than general elections also play their part. These include policy statements and factors which could influence a general election result.

3. Economic Influence

Other factors connected with the economy can affect share prices, particularly when they have a major impact on the money supply. The crash of October 1987 was triggered by fears about the US economy (see Chapter 15). Early in 1987 tax reform in the US provided much new money for investment, resulting in spectacular index increases.

Tax changes can also affect the economy by making investing in a particular way more or less attractive. Recent changes in stamp duty rates and the introduction of Personal Equity Plans are examples.

Tax reductions release more cash which is then available for more investment, which in turn tends to push up the prices. Changes in company taxation which mean that companies pay less tax, increase dividends and retained profit, which in turn also pushes up share prices.

Interest rate reductions make 'safer' investments less attractive and shares more attractive, which tends to push up prices. Also many smaller trading companies borrow, so an interest rate reduction is good news for them. For banks a reduction is not such good news, as that is where they earn most of their profits.

4. Other Influences

Changes in the law, international treaties and agreements, major strikes and the publication of economic statistics can also affect share prices. In exactly what way depends on the circumstances of the case, but each such example is usually well explained in the financial press at the time.

It is easy to be cynical and say that shares rose 'after the new OPEC agreement' (or whatever). Whether there is any real connection or not is immaterial, share prices move according to the *perception* of the economy. If the market-makers think something will affect the economy, they adjust their prices so that it does.

Recent examples of things which have favourably affected share prices are:

a CBI report that wage settlements are at a ten-year low; the Chancellor's favourable comments on the state of the pound;
a belief that bank rates will be reduced;
hopes that Germany and Japan will cut interest rates.

Examples of things which have adversely affected share prices in the last few years are:

the SDP–Liberal alliance improving in the pre-election polls;
uncertainties over the strength of the US dollar;
hints of a DTI investigation into takeovers;
Japan's call for talks on the dollar.

You will notice that hints and rumours are all it takes to influence prices. Major financial events, such as the Budget and the Autumn Statement, can influence prices for many weeks before and a few weeks after.

5. Miniskirts

A theory, included more for its entertainment value than its usefulness, is known as the 'hemline theory'.

This theory states that share prices move in concert with the hemlines on ladies' dresses. Despite its apparent fanciful nature, it has so far been very accurate; both the 1920s and the 1960s were bull periods (rising share prices).

It is known that people spend more money when they feel generally contented, and it is suggested that changes in fashion may be another manifestation of that same symptom.

Good weather, royal events and sporting victories also prompt the individual investor to spend, but as the individual investor still represents a minor part of the nation's investing population, such things still have a negligible effect on share prices.

Attempts have been made to link share prices with sun spots and phases of the moon. No success has yet been noted.

6. Influence on Companies

The share prices of a specific company, as opposed to the economy as a whole, can be affected by factors peculiar to the company's business or peculiar to the company itself.

These factors are more difficult to discern, which is where good research can make a great difference.

It is worth noting that not all countries react the same way to the same circumstances. For example, the AIDS scare boosted pharmaceutical shares in Japan, regardless of whether the particular companies were involved in research or not.

In the UK and US there was no such general boost, but companies known to have produced AIDS-controlling drugs enjoyed massive boosts. The announcement by BTP that its biocide 'Nipacide BTP' could kill the AIDS virus outside the body caused their shares to rocket from 162p to 255p before settling at 235p.

7. Influence on a Particular Trade

A whole trade is easily affected by some event which may appear irrelevant.

For example, when the US government bombed Libya, airline share prices fell. The reason is obvious to those who appreciate that travel to the Middle East is the second most lucrative market for the airlines (after US travel). There were widespread fears of reprisal attacks, which prompted people to stop flying, with the resultant loss of income.

Note that the fact that Libya did not retaliate is irrelevant. Share prices move according to the *perception* of the likely outcome. Here the perception was right in that passenger flights were badly hit by the fear of reprisals.

Another example is that tobacco companies currently show a low price/earnings ratio. They are regarded as a bad long-term investment as smoking declines in popularity, and as governments attack tobacco companies by imposing higher duties and restricting their advertising.

8. Influence of Company News

An individual company's share price is affected by any news (or rumour) that reflects on its profit, earned or to be earned. This includes the annual accounts.

Here any inside information is useful. This should be distinguished from *insider* information which is illegal.

There is, however, nothing illegal in noticing that a company seems to be in a healthy state because plenty of overtime is being worked, or the company is placing long-term orders, or the commission-only sales manager is looking at expensive houses in Esher. Charles Dow, who founded the *Wall Street Journal* and the *Dow–Jones Index*, made his fortune from investing in steel mills. He simply walked round the mills and counted the number of chimneys belching out smoke.

News of a major contract, or a scientific or technological breakthrough also pushes up prices. Takeovers, particularly contested ones, usually result in the target company's prices increasing sharply. As one bidder starts to emerge as the favourite, that company's share prices will also start to climb.

One of the biggest adverse influences is an investigation by the Department of Trade and Industry. This effectively states to the world that the company is suspected of a breach of company law. Management can become paralysed during the investigation, heads may roll, litigation may ensue and profitable but illegal practices may have to stop.

Other factors likely to affect a share price are news of an impending strike, the loss of a major customer or order, and litigation.

Technological developments which may threaten the marketability of a company's products, or a new competitor, rarely affect a share price as competition is seen as healthy and therefore desirable.

Changes in senior staff or company policy can affect share prices either way.

Again it must be stressed that the *perception* of the company is more relevant to share prices than the underlying reality. Rumours are more relevant than fact. When it was rumoured that a scandal about Burtons was to be published in a Sunday newspaper, the company's shares fell by 10 per cent almost immediately. The scandal concerned only the sex life of the company's chairman, which is unlikely to affect a company's commercial performance. The share price promptly recovered of course.

The scandal around Guinness concerned the company's attempt deliberately to manipulate its share price. Both Guinness and Argyll were bidding for control of Distillers by offering their shares in exchange for Distillers shares. Obviously the more valuable the offered shares were, the more likely a Distillers shareholder would be to accept the offer. So Guinness manipulated their share price upwards by creating an artificial shortage of them. This was done by persuading friendly institutions to buy large numbers of Guinness shares. These financial inducements were in clear breach of company law.

Guinness won control of Distillers. But when the truth was exposed, Guinness had to allow an extra £125m in its accounts to cover 'unusual transactions and arrangements'. The chairman and three other directors of Guinness resigned or were sacked as a result. Three people in other companies were sacked or asked to resign, and lawsuits and criminal proceedings began in what became the worst City scandal of recent years.

9. Bull and Bear Cycles

A *bull* period is when share prices are generally rising. A *bear* cycle is when they are generally falling.

Traditionally such periods were seen in cycles, where the bull period might last five years and the bear period a shorter time (it is harder to make money in a bear period).

However the economy was in one long bull period from 1975 to October 1987. It is too early to say whether the October 1987 crash is the start of a bear cycle or just the redressing of the year's earlier gains. The author inclines to the latter view, but he is not infallible!

In a bear cycle, the thing to remember is not to panic. Hold on to the shares you believe have underlying value and sell the rest. Buying traded options, and selling shares you do not own (in the hope that you can buy them for less when you need them) are extremely risky pursuits. Option dealing and bear buying can easily bankrupt you.

6. Understanding
The Financial Times

1. The Information Needed

The individual investor needs to know:

  i the quoted value of his shares,
  ii the state of the economy generally (as indicated by the FT indices),
  iii relevant comments that may appear about the company, its trade and the economy generally.

2. Share Information (Tuesday to Saturday)

Quoted companies have share details printed in *The Financial Times*, over several pages towards the back. Lists of the major companies also appear in *The Times*, *The Daily Telegraph*, *The London Daily News*, the *Guardian*, *The Independent* and *The London Standard*.

Details given below refer to *The Financial Times*. Other papers may give only part of the information.

Share details are listed under these nine columns:

High Low | Stock | Price | + or − | Div net | C'vr | Y'ld Grs | P/E

Stock gives you the name of the company and the type of share. One company may have more than one type of share. If only the company's name appears, it refers to an ordinary share with a nominal value of 25p. Nominal value is sometimes called 'par value'.

∥ by the price means no par value (not legal in the UK).

Other abbreviations used are:

'A' 'A' share
cap capital
cum cumulative
cnv, or cv covertible

30

do   ditto
ln   loan (stock)
pc   per cent
pf   preference
pref preference share
ptg   participating
vot   voting

Other symbols and abbreviations are explained in a table by the results.

Price gives the closing middle price of the previous day. This price takes account of any inter-office dealings after the Stock Exchange has closed.

The price is in pence unless another currency is denominated by its usual abbreviation. Sometimes symbols appear by the price. Their meaning is given below:

  #   share dealing suspended, the price is the last quoted before suspension.

  cd cum div (you are entitled to a dividend about to be declared)

  xd ex div (you are not entitled to a recently declared dividend).

High and **low** show the share price's highest and lowest prices so far during the year. At the beginning of the calendar year, this figure will actually refer to the high and low since the beginning of the previous calendar year (i.e. in the previous 12–16 months). It reverts to the high and low just for the current year in spring. The year or years to which the high and low refer is printed above the columns.

These columns give the investor some perspective on the share's movement. But such perspective should be seen in the context of how the market has moved generally.

* before a high or low means that the price has been adjusted in respect of a rights issue.

+ **or** **–** shows by how much the share price has moved since the close of the previous day's trading.

Div net This figure shows the rate of dividend paid in the latest year, expressed in pence per share with tax deducted at the basic rate.

The table by the results lists the many letters used by the dividend figures to indicate changes in interim payments, special payments and assumptions that have had to be made.

C'vr means dividend cover. As a rough rule, the higher this figure is, the more secure is the dividend. This is the net profit divided by the total amount of dividends. This is the number of times that the company could pay the same dividend from its profits.

If this figure is less than 1.0, it means that the company is using past profits to pay its current dividend. If this figure is high (say, above 4.0), it indicates that the company is retaining much of its profits, probably for some major expansion of its activities.

Y'ld gr's shows the gross dividend yield. This figure indicates how the market views that share. If it believes that the company will be prosperous, the share value is likely to be high, pushing the dividend down. Generally the *lower* this figure is, the better. It is the yield (dividend expressed as a percentage of the share price) grossed up to indicate the amount an investor is deemed to have received before basic rate income tax was deducted at source. The grossing up percentage is $\frac{100}{BR}$ where BR is the basic rate of income tax (29 per cent to 5 April 1987, then 27 per cent).

The percentage is then comparable with gross return percentages from other investments.

P/E indicates the price/earnings ratio. This ratio used to be regarded as the most important single indicator of how a company was performing: the higher the figure, the better. It is the price of the share divided by its earnings per share figure for the last twelve months. The figure for 'earnings per share' is one which the company itself must declare in its accounts. It must be calculated in accordance with the detailed procedure given in the Statement of Standard Accounting Practice 3 (SSAP 3). Despite this, the stated figure can sometimes be misleading (possibly deliberately so) and for this reason *The Financial Times* sometimes recalculates the company's figures. It says that this policy 'has been known to cause apoplexy among financial directors'.

From 1980 onwards, companies' accounts have had to comply with SSAP 15. This allowed financial directors some new scope as to how much tax they showed in the accounts. This introduced a new subjectivity into the accounts which tended to reduce the significance of the ratio. For some banks, insurance companies, investment trusts and mining companies, the subjectivity is so great that the figure is often not given at all.

3. Share Information (Monday)

As the Stock Exchange does not trade on a Saturday, Monday's edition of *The Financial Times* reprints the share prices of the previous Friday.

It makes two changes to how these are reported however:

    i the 'high' and 'low' columns are replaced with a column stating the months in which the dividends are paid. There will usually be two months indicated, usually six months apart.

    ii the '+ or –' column is replaced by one marked 'xd'. This is followed by a date, and refers to when a new buyer could last buy a share without entitlement to the last dividend.

4. Interpretation

You are likely only to be interested in the price of the share, and may choose to ignore the other statistical information.

However, price statistics by themselves only tell part of the story. They tell you that a share has gone up or down, and give you numerical indications of how the market sees that share, but these statistics do not tell you why any of these things have happened.

To obtain this information, it is necessary to read the report published each day (except Monday) just before the share prices. This report, written by the *Financial Times'* own reporters, gives a clear indication of which of the many movements in prices and indicies are significant, and what reasons lie behind those moves. Regular reading of this report is probably the quickest way to understanding how the markets respond.

Additional statistical information is given in various 'boxes'. The most useful to the small investor will be the various indices calculated by the newspaper and explained below.

5. Indices

Despite references to the 'Financial Times index', the newspaper actually publishes many indices.

The most widely used are:

    i Financial Times 30-share index,
   ii Financial Times–Stock Exchange 100 index,
  iii Financial Times–Actuaries indices.

Other indices are calculated for other markets.

The New York Stock Exchange's equivalent is the Dow–Jones index, and Tokyo's equivalent is the Nikkei–Dow market index. Both of these are reported in *The Financial Times*.

6. Financial Times 30-share Index

The Financial Times 30-share index is the oldest index (it was introduced in 1935) and is still the most popular. It is quoted on the news almost like a religious devotion, yet few people really understand its purpose.

The index is calculated by taking *only 30 share prices*. These are companies which are chosen as being representative of the market as a whole.

During its existence, the index has sought to reflect the change in the nation's economy by occasionally changing a constituent member. Thus there has been a move away from heavy manufacturing industries to service companies and the oil industry. In December 1984 the National Westminster Bank was included, prior to which the index had been known as the Financial Times Industrial Ordinary Share Index. Despite the change, seven of the original class of 30 from 1935 are still in the index.

Originally this index was calculated once a day. It is now calculated throughout the day, though the closing index is still the most widely used.

For those of you who want to understand the technicalities, the constituent share prices are expressed as base figures (similar to a percentage) and the *geometric* mean is calculated. This is done by *multiplying* the bases and taking the thirtieth root. An average (or *arithmetic* mean) would add them and divide by 30.

The effect of using a geometric mean is that the index

shows the overall movements *relative to each other*. If one company's share price doubled and another halved, their geometric mean would remain unchanged, but the arithmetic mean would show a 25 per cent increase, as illustrated below:

> A and B each have a share price of 100p. The geometric and arithmetic means are both 100p. A doubles to 200p, B halves to 50p.
> The geometric mean is $\sqrt{200 \times 50} = \sqrt{10,000} = 100$ (unchanged)
> The arithmetic mean is $\dfrac{50 + 200}{2} = 125$ (increased by 25
>
> per cent)

The index is intended to measure the 'mood' of the market – as to how optimistic or pessimistic (bullish or bearish) it is believed to be.

As a long-term indicator, it tends to understate the market's movements. This is partly a mathematical quality of geometric means, and partly reflects the fact that spectacular growth is more likely to be found in the smaller companies outside the 30 constituents.

The companies in the FT 30-share index are:

Allied–Lyons	Glaxo
ASDA–MFI	Grand Metropolitan
Beecham Group	Guinness
BICC	Hanson Trust
Blue Circle Industries	Hawker Siddeley
BOC Group	ICI
BTR	Lucas Industries
Boots	Marks and Spencer
British Gas	National Westminster Bank
British Petroleum	P & O
British Telecom	Plessey
Cadbury Schweppes	Royal Insurance
Courtaulds	Tate and Lyle
GEC	Thorn EMI
GKN	Trusthouse Forte

7. Financial Times–Stock Exchange 100 Index

This index is more commonly known as FT–SE 100 index. With the Stock Exchange's usual penchant for silly terms, it has also become known as 'Footsie'.

The index was introduced in February 1984 (at a base of 1000) to indicate the movement of the one hundred largest companies (measured by market capitalisation) regardless of the nature of their business. Channel 4 News variously describes the index as 'broader based' and 'more representative' than the 30-share index. The first description is correct, the second is not.

Apart from using more companies and making these simply the largest companies rather than choosing a representative selection, one of the main advantages of this index is that it is updated on a minute-to-minute basis, thus effectively providing a continuous index during trading hours.

Apart from the differences stated, this index is calculated in the same way as the 30-share index.

8. Financial Times–Actuaries Share Indices

As different sectors of the economy will perform differently, the listed companies are classified under generic headings and sub-headings.

The main headings are known as equity groups, and the sub-headings are known as sub-equity groups. They are:

1 capital goods, comprising:
2 building materials
3 contracting, construction etc
4 electricals
5 electronics
6 mechanical engineering
8 metals and metal forming
9 motors
10 other industrial materials

21 consumer groups, comprising:
22 brewers and distillers
25 food manufacturing
26 food retailing
27 health and household products
29 leisure

31 packaging and paper
32 publishing and printing
34 stores
35 textiles

40 other groups, comprising:
41 agencies
42 chemicals
43 conglomerates
45 shipping and transport
47 telephone networks
48 miscellaneous

This list is then itself summarised as '49 Industrial group'.
Another equity sub-group is '51 oil and gas', which, when added to 'industrial group' gives the 500-share index.

There is also '61 Financial group' which comprises:
62 banks
65 insurance (life)
66 insurance (composite)
67 insurance (brokers)
68 merchant banks
69 property
70 other financial

And outside any group are:
71 investment trusts
81 mining finance
91 overseas traders.

All these are summarised as *the all-share index*.

Every other week or so, companies are added or removed from the list. Occasionally the sub-groups themselves are changed (which partly explains the missing numbers). After each group or sub-group name and number, another number in brackets indicates how many companies constitute the group or sub-group. There are about 730 companies that make up the all-share index.

The indices were each introduced at 100 on 10 April 1962 (or when the sub-group was first constituted if later). *The Financial Times* states that the indices are compiled 'through the use of elegant and complex mathematical formulae'. This elegant complexity gives *arithmetic* means (unlike the other indices) adjusted for companies leaving or joining sub-groups.

The information is presented daily in a big table which shows for each sub-group:

  i the index number
  ii the change since the previous index, expressed as a percentage,
  iii estimated earnings yield (expressed as a percentage)
  iv gross dividend yield (expressed as a percentage of the average yield dividend by the sector's market capitalisation, and grossed up assuming deduction of income tax at the basic rate),
  v estimated P/E ratio. This is calculated as a weighted average within the group using only the 'net basis' for determining earnings per share. The 'net basis' gives a lower figure than the alternative 'nil basis' as it excludes tax which is irrecoverable because of the size of the dividend.

There are also comparative indices for each of the previous three days and for one year previously.

Every quarter, valuation tables are published which give market capitalisation figures for each sub-group, both as an amount and as a percentage of the whole market.

These indices allow you to discover how well your shares are performing by comparing them with others in the same equity group.

9. Other Indices

The Financial Times also publishes a simpler table of these additional indices:

  i government securities
  ii fixed interest
  iii gold mines

of which the first is the most widely used, as a measure of the gilts market.

The same table gives statistical information on Stock Exchange activity, including the number of bargains, how many shares were traded, etc.

Other indices are published for overseas markets, and for options, futures, unit trusts and commodities.

Separate lists show recent issues, rights offers, trading volumes, and rises and falls by equity group.

On 21 March 1987, the newspaper launched The FT-Actuaries World Indices. This innovation comprises over 1000 indices from 23 countries, 9 regions, 36 groups and 7 broad economic sectors, drawn from 2400 'globally investable equity securities'. The indices use arithmetic averages, with 31 December 1986 providing the base of 100. The indices are used as the other FT indices, but for overseas and multinational shares.

10. Other Economic Indicators

The economy is not measured just in stock market indices.

To gain a more complete picture, it is necessary also to consider:

   i the retail price index,
   ii interest rates,
   iii the exchange rate,
   iv money supply figures, and
   v gold and oil prices.

This list is indicative, not exhaustive. These measures allow you to assess the general state of the economy as explained in Chapter 5, section 4 'Other influences'.

The retail price index is calculated as a weighted arithmetic mean to indicate the relative cost of typical retail expenditure. The index was 100 in January 1974. This means that in January 1985, when the index stood at 359.8, retail prices were on average 3½ times what they were eleven years earlier. With the curious exception of mortgage interest, the index does not include finance charges. The traditional method of calculating the rate of inflation is the percentage increase in the index from a year earlier.

Interest rates are based on what the banks charge for lending money to each other. The most important of these is known as LIBOR (London Inter-Bank Offered Rate) for three months. For the rest of us, banks quote a base rate (which has been in the order of 10–11 per cent in recent years) from which other rates are determined.

The exchange rate is how much foreign currency can be acquired for one pound sterling. The spot rate also gives (cautious) indications of how the pound is expected to fare in one and three months' time. There is the 'sterling index' which measure the value of the pound against other currencies, weighted according to how much business this country does with them.

Money supply figures indicate the size of the whole economy. They are measured by reference to abbreviations:

M0 = notes and coins and banks' balances with the Bank of England,

M1 = notes and coins, and current account balances of private sector residents held in sterling,

M2 = M1 plus sterling deposit accounts of private sector UK residents,

M3 = M2 plus deposit accounts with other banks, non-sterling deposits of the private sector and all deposits of the public sector.

M0 is sometimes called 'narrow money' and is comparatively unimportant. M2 has become so unimportant it is no longer even reported.

M3 is the commonest indicator. In 1987 the Chancellor finally abandoned setting a target for M3. Too fast an expansion of the money supply leads to inflation.

Oil and gold are two minerals on which much of the economy is based. Until 1931 all monetary units were largely equated with the value of gold. It has reduced in importance since then, though it is still used to settle debts between countries. Oil is important for the different reason that so much of the nation's economy is affected by the price of oil.

The commonest units of measure for these minerals are 1 troy oz of gold and 1 barrel (35 gallons) of crude oil from Brent oil field, payable at 15 days.

7. Choosing Your Shares

1. Preliminaries

The decision on which shares to buy depends on many factors such as:

    i your need for capital growth rather than investment income,

   ii the degree of risk you are prepared to take,

 iii the time you can wait for the investment to show a return,

 iv in what sectors of the economy you wish to invest (either because you have particular knowledge in one area, or because you are opposed to, or specifically wish to encourage, a certain sector or sectors).

All this presupposes that you have a good working knowledge of the economy generally (that you keep yourself up to date on what is happening in the world), and have understood all that we have said so far.

If this is not so, you will probably be better off with a unit trust or managed portfolio for the time being. There is plenty of time to learn more.

In discussing what shares to buy, we have assumed that you are going to deal with shares rather than other types of security or investment. This aspect of the decision-making process is discussed more fully in Chapter 13.

Many of the comments in Chapter 8 about *when* to buy shares are equally helpful in deciding what to buy.

2. Choosing the Shares

There are over 7000 shares quoted on the Stock Exchange. A glance at the last few pages of any day's *Financial Times* will give you an idea of the size of the task.

However, some categorisation has already been done to assist you.

An obvious category for you may be a particular sector of the economy. If you have experience of the oil industry, or electronics, or publishing, or building, it makes sense to invest accordingly as you will understand the implications to that sector of what you read in the news.

After the sector, the next most important factor is size. Shares are already classified as alpha, beta, gamma and delta shares. It is unlikely that the small investor will invest in gamma and delta shares.

Alpha shares are among 'blue chip' shares. These are of companies, often household names, of large size, steady growth, with plenty of asset backing and a good dividend record.

Currently the alpha shares include:

Allied–Lyons	Coats Viyella
Amstrad	Commercial Union
Argyll Group	Consolidated Goldfields
ASDA–MFI	Cookson
Associated British Foods	Courtaulds
Barclays Bank	Dee Corporation
Bass	Dixons Group
BAT	English China Clays
Beecham	Fisons
BET	GEC
Blue Circle	General Accident
BOC	GKN
Boots	Glaxo
BPB Industries	Globe Investment
BPCC	Granada
British Aerospace	Grand Metropolitan
British Airways	Hotels
British and	GRE
Commonwealth	Guinness
British Gas	GUS 'A'
British Petroleum	Hanson Trust
British Telecom	Hawker Siddeley
Britoil	Hillsdown Holdings
BTR	ICI
Bunzl	Jaguar
Burton	Ladbroke
Cable and Wireless	Land Securities
Cadbury Schweppes	Legal and General

Lloyds Bank
Lonrho
Marks and Spencer
MEPC
Midland Bank
National Westminster
    Bank
Next
Pearson
P and O deferred
Pilkington Brothers
Plessey
Prudential
Racal
Rank Organisation
Reckitt & Coleman
Redland
Reed International
Reuters
RHM
RMC
Rolls-Royce
Rowntree Mackintosh
Royal Bank of Scotland
Royal Insurance

RTZ
Saatchi
Sainsbury
Scottish and Newcastle
Sears
Sedgwick
Shell Transport
Smith and Nephew
Standard Chartered
    Group
STC
Storehouse
Sun Alliance
Tarmac
Tesco
Thorn EMI
Trafalgar House
Trustee Savings Bank
Trusthouse Forte
Unigate
Unilever
United Biscuits
Wellcome Foundation
Whitbread 'A'
Woolworth

3. Methods of Choosing

Traditionally a portfolio should includes at least one 'safe' share. This will usually be a 'blue chip' company, probably a constituent of the FT-30 share index. Sometimes a gilt is included instead.

Thereafter we are looking for 'volatility'. This means shares that are moving up and down. A simple way of spotting such shares is to look in *The Financial Times* (or other newspaper) to see what shares have a wide difference between the 'High' and 'Low' for the year.

These shares can then be monitored for a while, using either the moving averages method or charting methods described in Chapters 8 and 9.

Another method is to take a long-term view by looking up the highs and lows from previous years and plotting each of them on a graph where the *y*-axis (vertical) is in a logarithmic scale. This means that instead of going 1, 2, 3, 4, 5, etc. it goes 1, 2, 4, 8, 16, etc. The reason is that we are not seeking to measure the *amount* by which the share price moves, but the *ratio* by which it moves, i.e. has it increased by 50 per cent? If you really want to be clever, you can always buy logarithmic graph paper for the purpose. The most volatile shares will be those where the gap between the lines is widening. For sources of information see section 6 of this chapter.

A short cut is simply to look for shares with a wide gap between the high and low figures and buy those whose current prices are near the low, and hope for the best. You are trading some accuracy for expediency.

It should be stressed here that volatility means that the shares are prone to go down quickly as well as to go up quickly.

It is advisable to diversify to the extent of ensuring that the shares are not always in the same sector, e.g. they are not all in electronics or construction.

If all this sounds too much trouble, shares can simply be chosen at random. This may seem like a complete cop-out, but actually such portfolios have often been known to perform better than the FT 30-share index.

4. Ethical Investment

You may have strong views about certain activities and decide that you are therefore not going to invest in certain companies. This is known as 'ethical investment'.

Your stockbroker will often be able to advise you about what the company actually does. Alternatively you can find out by writing to EIRIS (Ethical Investment Research and Information Service), 9 Poland Street, London W1V 3DG. *tel*: 01-439 2772.

They are still a small operation but have details on over 500 companies. Information is supplied in fact-sheets supplied on annual subscription starting at £35 a year. A newsletter is also published.

There are currently three ethical unit trusts:

Ethical Investment Trust, 10 Queen Street, London W1X 7PD

Fellowship Trust, Buckmaster and Moore, Stock
Exchange, London EC2P 2JT
Stewardship Unit Trust, Friends Provident, Pixham End,
Dorking, Surrey RH4 1QA

The usual exclusions are those companies which
manufacture arms, alcoholic drink or tobacco products, which
operate gambling establishments, and which trade in South
Africa. The Fellowship Trust invests in UK and overseas
companies, the other two just in UK companies.

By excluding companies and thus limiting one's choice, it
could be presumed that an ethical portfolio or unit trust
would perform less well than an unrestricted portfolio.
Curiously, ethical unit trusts have tended to perform slightly
better. A suggested reason for this is that the extra attention
given to the companies in general has resulted in wiser
investment decisions.

Ethical portfolios can also include companies which are
seen to be helping needy areas of society or helping relieve
Third World poverty. The main public company is Traidcraft
which markets goods produced in such countries. But only
buy Traidcraft shares for ethical reasons – not to make a
profit.

In the United States, ethical investment is believed to
account for 10 per cent of all private investment, and still to
be growing in importance. It is believed that ethical
investment will become more popular in the UK also.

5. 'Sid's' Shares

Although it is impossible for a book like this to comment on
many shares in any detail, brief comments are given below on
four popular privatisation shares:

> **British Airways** like all airlines is a volatile share, and
> not suitable for those who have no other shareholdings.
> As airlines go, it is considered a good investment.

> **British Gas**, as the biggest ever flotation, was hyped
> heavily, but the £41m spent on advertising told us little
> as to *why* the shares should be bought. It is difficult to
> see that the nation's gas supply provides any basis for
> useful growth, and the share price is being kept high by
> sentiment rather than intrinsic worth.

British Telecom was a deservedly popular investment. The company has shown its ability to adapt to commercial reality. It is well placed to compete with Mercury as the latter develops, and has excellent potential in a high growth market.

The Trustee Savings Bank has shown itself capable of competing with the big banks. Unlike them it is not straddled with Third World debt, and, being smaller, has more growth potential.

6. Sources of Information

Information on daily share prices is published in *The Times*, *The Daily Telegraph*, *The Financial Times*, the *Guardian*, *The Independent* and *The London Standard*. Useful weekly summaries are contained in *The Sunday Times* and *The Sunday Telegraph*.

There are many useful magazines on the market. *Investors Chronicle* does not give share prices as such, but gives extensive coverage of a good range of companies in each issue, plus general advice, including material written for the beginner. *Money Observer* is another magazine which gives general guidance on financial matters. *Money Week* is specifically aimed at financial intermediaries.

Back copies of *The Financial Times* can be obtained from the larger libraries. Copies of the main newspapers going back several years can be found in specialist libraries such as City Business Library, Gilbert House, 55 Basinghall Street, London EC2V 5BX (*tel*: 01-638 8215). Access to copies is also available from the British Library Newspaper Library, Colindale Avenue, London NW9 (*tel*: 01-200 5515).

For isolated pieces of information, *The Financial Times* offers a free service on 01-236 1340, but the information you can get on this number is very restricted. *The Daily Telegraph* offers an excellent information service (not just on financial matters). You ring 01-353 4242 and ask for Information.

If you subscribe to Ceefax, Oracle or Teletext, current stock prices can be paged on them.

It should be remembered, though, that while odd pieces of information can usually be obtained free, more extensive information is expensive. A year's subscription to *Investors Chronicle* will cost you about £50. A year's subscription to *The Financial Times* (40p a day) is about £130. These figures can easily eat up the profit of a small investment.

If you are doing really well and have the need for a full service, you can subscribe to the Financial Times Business Information Service which gives you free access to their massive library facilities. The service costs £775 a year. The librarians' time is charged at £48 an hour. Copies of annual reports are supplied at £12 each (they are free if you write to the actual company itself). The service was established in 1971.

It is advisable to ask your stockbroker what information he will provide you with.

8. When to Buy and Sell

1. General Considerations

Shares can be chosen for buying and selling by various methods:

    i following advice,
    ii analysis of track record (known as 'fundamental analysis'),
    iii criterion selection.

The selection process needs to consider risk and need. At its simplest, the greater the risk you are prepared to take, the greater the potential gain. Your money could grow three- or four-fold in a year, or you could lose the lot.

If you want safety, you can buy a unit trust or shares in a safe but unspectacular company like Marks and Spencer. If you want risk, you can try a small company, perhaps a penny share, or provide venture capital or buy traded options. These are considered in greater detail in Chapter 13. Considerations for an initial portfolio are discussed in Chapter 7. A general discussion on what causes share prices to move is given in Chapter 5.

Before committing your money to any investment, it may be worth trying a 'dry run'. A dry run should be done for at least ten weeks, preferably longer. If you cannot wait that long, then put some of your money (no more than a third) into a unit trust or 'blue chip' company *and monitor that as well as your dummy investments.*

In a dry run, you apply your judgement to a share portfolio without actually buying the shares and see how your 'investment' would have done. Thus you gain the experience without risking any money.

2. Advice

Advice on what shares to buy and sell can be found in:

    i tipsheets (such as *Stock Market Confidential*),
    ii newspapers (such as *The Sunday Telegraph*) and
    iii newsletters from brokers.

Sources of information are discussed in Chapter 7, section 6.

Such advice can be useful if considered properly. A cynic may ask, if these people know so much about the stock market, why don't they play the market themselves instead of telling everyone else?

The commonest complaints against such advice are:

    i the advisers tell you what to buy and when, but never tell you when to sell,
    ii the advisers never give you any track record to show you how good (or otherwise) *they* are, and
    iii everyone else gets the same advice, and that in itself can influence the share price.

The last point is perhaps the most pertinent. All the market-makers also read the newspapers, newsletters and tipsheets. If a company is recommended and enough people follow that advice, the rule of supply and demand will cause that share price to rise. The naïve investor will see this as proof that the advice was correct, rather than as an obvious example of self-fulfilment. He may learn that lesson the hard way when he comes to sell the shares.

Any such short-term effect described above is only likely to last for the period of account (two weeks). If you really believe that the advice is sound, instead of buying, you may choose to wait the two weeks, to the next account, to see if the price has reduced after the initial interest. Such a share may then become a good bargain as disillusioned buyers seek to sell – thus forcing down the price. When this book has become a bestseller and everyone is waiting two weeks before buying tipped shares, you will need to develop a new strategy!

The best advice is that which is supported by argument. You can then weigh up the merits of the argument against your own understanding, and nothing can beat your own understanding!

The leading tipsheets are probably:

> *Stock Market Confidential*, Stonehart Publications Ltd,
> 57–61 Mortimer Street, London W1N 7TD. This
> weekly publication *does* give track records of its
> recommendations, and does tell you when to sell
> what it has previously recommended you buy.

> *New Issue Share Guide*, 3 Fleet Street, London EC4Y 1AU.
> Published at least once a month, claims successes 9
> times out of 10. Subscription gives you a free book
> and access to a daily recorded summary by telephone.

> *Penny Share Focus*, 11 Blomfield Street, London EC2M
> 7AY. Published monthly and including a monitoring
> service.

Stockbrokers' newsletters are sometimes regarded as offering
a better quality of advice. First the stockbroker's reputation
(and hence his trading ability) is on the line, and secondly the
advice is given to a much more restricted audience, with the
result that the advice itself will have little or no effect on the
share price.

Better still is the personal advice obtained from the
stockbroker, but remember that the cleverest analyst will
never be right all the time, so don't abandon your own
understanding altogether.

3. Track Record

A company's track record can give an idea as to its future
prospects. Most public companies will provide you with a free
copy of their last published accounts on written request to the
company secretary. These accounts are likely to contain a five-
or ten-year summary.

There are ways of calculating ratios (by dividing one
number in the accounts by another) which can be compared
with other companies, industry norms and previous years.
This is known as 'fundamental analysis'.

But all this is likely to be a fruitless task for the investor.
Accounts are rarely published sooner than four months after

the year-end, so you can be looking at information up to sixteen months old.

The analysis has effectively already been done anyway, by people who had that information (and probably acted upon it) before you ever saw it.

More detailed information exists in other forms, such as Extel cards. Your stockbroker may be willing to supply copies to you. Many libraries will have back copies of *The Financial Times* and the *Stock Exchange Daily Official List*. Information is also given on Prestel, Oracle and Ceefax.

4. Analysis of Share Price

Analysis of share price covers a range of activities designed to predict future share movement on the basis of past movement.

The two commonest methods are:

   i moving average, and
 ii charting.

5. Moving Averages

The object of share dealing is to buy when the shares are at their cheapest and sell when they are at their highest. It must be stated at the outset that no one will ever do this perfectly. If you buy at 10 per cent above the lowest price and sell at 10 per cent less than the highest, you have done very well. If you sell at a good profit, the fact that the share price carries on rising afterwards should not bother you. You must always concentrate on what you *have* achieved, and not worry about what you *might* have achieved.

Looking at share movements by themselves is not always helpful, as the movements can be subject to various short-term fluctuations which make it hard to discern a general trend. The moving average method smooths out such short-term trends.

Imagine a share whose prices over 17 weeks were:

804 371 661 726 437 556 783 503 577 723 569 589 672 644 600 640 810

How is it doing? Its final price is only 6p above the opening price, so should we sell it then or not?

It is not easy to see any pattern here. Showing it on a graph helps little either (Fig. 1).

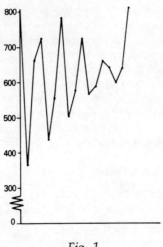

Fig. 1

If, instead, we calculate the averages for three weeks at a time, the figures become:

600 612 586 608 615 592 614 621 601 623 627 610 635 642 628 650

and the peaks on the graph become less marked (Fig. 2).

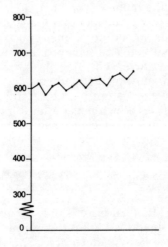

Fig. 2

If we take nine-weekly averages, the figures become:

600 602 603 605 607 609 612 615 617 620 624 629 635 640

which on the graph gives us a smooth curve (Fig. 3).

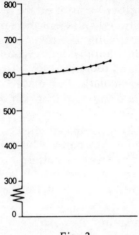

Fig. 3

We can see that the underlying trend of the shares is a gradual increase in value. The figure of 640 is an average of nine weeks and therefore is equivalent to a current figure 4½ weeks old. If we were to project the smooth curve for 4½ weeks, we would have a projected current average of about 675, so a price of 810 would represent a good profit.

The use of moving averages in record-keeping is discussed in Chapter 9.

6. Charting

The disadvantages of using moving averages are determining the length over which to calculate the average, and spotting the underlying trend. Such underlying trends will inevitably be historical.

But even from the graph in Figure 1, it can be seen that the troughs are gradually increasing, indicating an upward trend (see 'ii resistance line' below).

Charting aims to see what the share price is going to do next according to the picture it draws on the graph.

Remember that share prices are governed by *perceived* value, which allows self-fulfilling predictions. It is also only fair to say that some analysts do not believe in charting at all. They believe that shares generally move without any regard to what they have done before. This is known as the 'random walk theory'. On the other hand, it ought to be stated that chartists have demonstrated sufficient measure of success to regard their methods as being worthy of explanation.

The methods are quite simple, just involving plotting share prices as a line graph and looking at the pictures. Many modern computers (particularly Apple MacIntosh and the Xerox Documenter) have software that will draw these graphs for you.

The pattern of fluctuations reflects the conflicting views of market-makers regarding the shares. The reasoning behind why such views lead to particular patterns and what the investor should do, is rather academic. It is sufficient for the investor to be able to recognise the pattern and know what to do.

The pictures have acquired names.

i Support line. A horizontal line can be drawn below which the share price never falls but keeps 'bouncing' off (see Fig. 4). The best time to buy is when the shares have just started to bounce up again; the best time to sell is when the shares are, say, 20 per cent above the resistance level, or have just started a downward turn. Traditionally such a share price only bounces up to five times before starting another pattern.

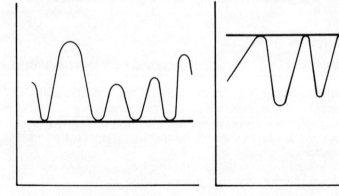

Fig. 4 Support line   *Fig. 5 Resistance line*

ii Resistance line. A horizontal line can be drawn above which the share price never rises. (See Fig. 5.) This is, in effect, the opposite to the support line, and the reverse rules apply. Sell as the shares start to move down from the resistance line; buy when they are, say, 20 per cent below or start to move up. Traditionally such a share price bounces up to the line no more than four times before drawing a different pattern. Some chartists prefer to wait a little when the shares move up to see whether the resistance line is penetrated.

iii Penetration of a support line. When the support line is penetrated, this is bad news and the shares should be sold (Fig. 6). Everyone else will be selling too of course and such a large sale will push the price even further down. You might choose to await a slight recovery in the price if you failed to get out early enough.

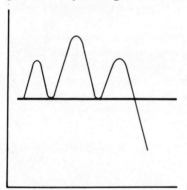

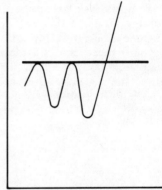

Fig. 6 Penetration of a support line

Fig. 7 Penetration of a resistance line

iv Penetration of a resistance line. Usually good news. It is a signal to hold shares and possibly buy more (Fig. 7).

v Support becomes resistance. When a horizontal line which acted as a support becomes a resistance line, the company is regarded as in serious trouble, and the usual course of action is to sell (Fig. 8). This can become yet another self-fulfilling prediction which results in the shares being marked down below their intrinsic value. If you believe this, you can hold the shares or possibly even buy more at discount prices, but be careful. Even if you are right, it is likely to take a while before the market generally regains its confidence, begins to agree with you and the shares can be profitably sold.

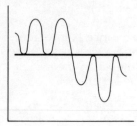

Fig. 8 *Support becomes resistance*

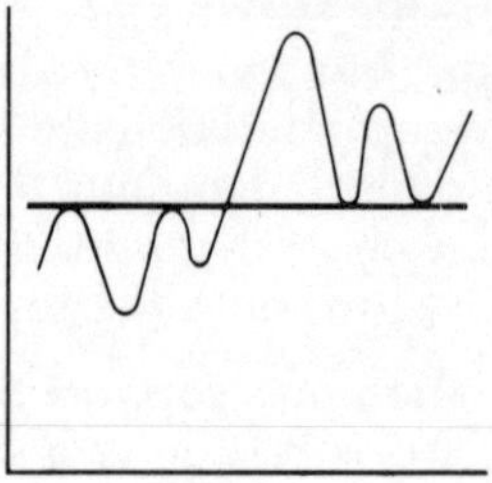

Fig. 9 *Resistance becomes support*

vi Resistance becomes support. This phenomenon is fairly common (Fig. 9). The line which provided the resistance becomes a support line and the shares bounce back to it, perhaps twice, before continuing a general upward trend. The shares are bought when the price has bounced back to the line. They are sold when they start to turn down, when a new pattern emerges, or when a predetermined margin has been reached. There is rarely any pressing need to sell.

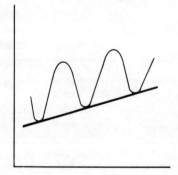

Fig. 10 *Upward trend*

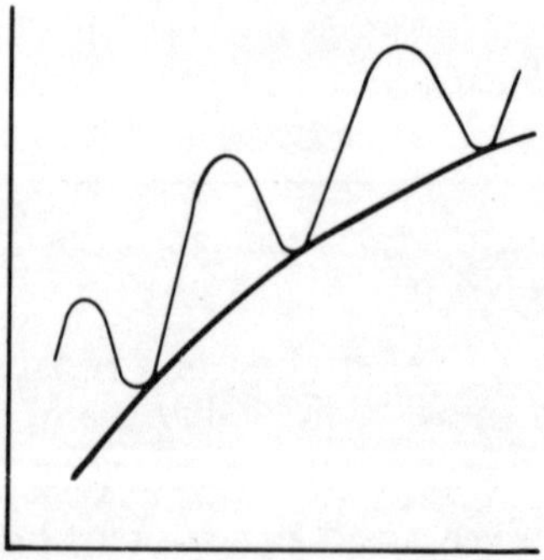

Fig. 11 *Curved support line – face up*

vii Upward trend. The upward trend is an upward sloping support line (Fig. 10). A bounce up from the line is the time to buy. It is usually prudent to wait a little while to see that this really is a bounce up, and that the line is not about to be penetrated.

There is no need to sell a share at all during an upward trend, but if you do want to sell, the best time is when the price is about 15 per cent above the support line or when the value starts to turn down again.

Instead of being straight, the line could be curved. This affects the degree to which the upward trend is expected to continue, as will easily be seen by projecting the curve. If the curve faces up (Fig. 11), the upward trend will peter out; if the curve faces down (Fig. 12), buy like mad.

Fig. 12 Curved support line – face down

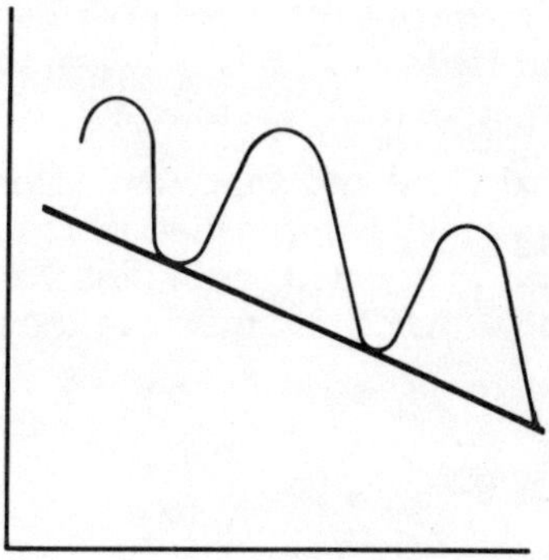

Fig. 13 Downward trend

viii Downward trend. Immediately this trend is spotted, the shares should be sold, as traditionally the trend (unlike its upward counterpart) tends to keep going longer.

Like the upward trend, the line could be curved rather than straight. If the curve faces down, the downward trend is dying out and the shares may even recover. If the curve faces up, sell quickly.

ix Upward channel. This comprises upward support and resistance lines between which the share price bounces. Marginal profits can be made during the bounces, but generally the shares are held until the pattern changes (Fig. 14).

A channel is sometimes called a 'trend line'.

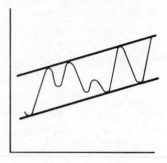

Fig. 14 Upward channel

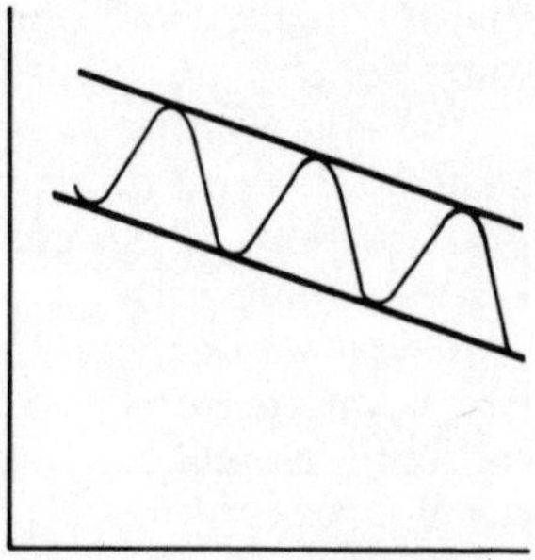

Fig. 15 Downward channel

x Downward channel. This comprises downward support and resistance lines between which the share price bounces (Fig. 15). It is generally advisable to sell such shares.

xi Head and shoulders. This pattern shows a line (the 'neckline') being penetrated, used as a support line twice, and then penetrated again (Fig. 16). The second penetration is the cue to sell. Only then can the pattern be clearly identified.

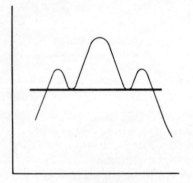

Fig. 16 Head and shoulders

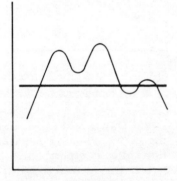

Fig. 17 Double top

xii Double top. This is similar to the head and shoulders, except that the second fall goes below the previous trough (Fig. 17). In fact the shares have simply peaked, with a hiccup in the process. The downward trend is the cue to sell.

xiii Double bottom. This is simply the double top in reverse; the second trough is less deep than the first (Fig. 18). The turn from the second trough is the time to buy. If feeling prudent, sell these shares when you have made 20 or 25 per cent, as the upward bounce could be short-lived.

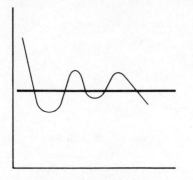

Fig. 18 Double bottom   Fig. 19 Flag

xiv Flag. A flag is a downward resistance line and an upward support line (Fig. 19). While the shares are bouncing within the resulting flag shape, the shares are regarded as being neither worth selling nor buying. The aim is to see whether the prices shoot up (buy) or down (sell) at the end of the flag. A hint can sometimes be detected if either line increases its upward or downward trend. This makes the picture of the flag point up or down, which is the direction the shares are expected to go when the flag ends.

7. Computer Programs

The recording and analysis of share movements can be effectively managed by computer. At present the author knows of three suitable programs.

Microvest+ is supplied by Brian Millard Investment Services, 16 Queensgate, Bramhall, Stockport, Cheshire: 061–439 3926. It will run on most common PCs and the Amstrad 8000 series PCW. Reasonably priced.

Stockmarket is supplied by Meridian Software, 38 Balcaskie Road, London SE9 1HQ: 01–850 7057. Reasonably priced.

Sharemaster is supplied by Synergy Software, 7 Hillside Road, Harpenden, Herts: 05827 2977. The firm is moving to Luton. Reasonably priced. The suppliers claim that their program is the most sophisticated.

The author has not seen or tried any of these programs and can give no guarantee or recommendation regarding them.

9. Keeping a Record

1. Introduction

You need to keep two sorts of records:

    i financial accounts, to record your profits and loss on share dealings, and

    ii management accounts, to help you decide what to buy and sell.

2. Financial Accounts

Many book-keeping textbooks suggest elaborate systems for keeping financial accounts, and many elaborate systems are on the market. In practice it is rarely necessary to acquire more stationery than one cash book.

The most widely available books are the Cathedral Analysis Books produced by Collins and available from larger stationers. They have markings like '3/9' which means that the left-hand page has three columns and the right-hand page has nine columns.

On the left-hand pages, you record your receipts; on the right-hand pages you record your expenditure.

It is necessary to distinguish between capital, income and overheads. It is also necessary to include sufficient details by each entry to know what each refers to.

The left-hand page columns may be headed:

Date Details Number Bank Capital Dividend Other

'Details' will give the name of the company and number and description of the shares.

'Number' refers to the contract note or other piece of paper with the details of the transaction. This is a number that you write on the document for filing purposes. You usually start from 1 upwards (regardless of whether they are for buying or selling). This number is known as the folio number. There are plenty of more elaborate systems available, but they are not necessary. The documents themselves are filed separately in some purpose-designed container (such as a shoe box) in number order.

'Bank' records all sums received and paid into the bank. Such sums are analysed between 'capital' (proceeds of selling shares), 'dividends' (the net amount received) and 'other' (anything else, e.g. refund of commission). There is usually no need to keep a separate column for the tax credit on dividends as this can easily be calculated at the year-end.

The right-hand page columns may be headed:

Date   Details   Number   Bank   Shares   Other

These details will be the equivalent of those on the left-hand page, except that 'shares' will indicate the total consideration paid, and there will be various columns categorising other items of expenses. These may include postage and stationery, magazines and other journals (including this book), computer software, etc. *(See examples on page 169.)*

There is no need to analyse the expenses of sales and purchases. It honestly does not matter at all how much stamp duty, commission, VAT, etc. you have paid. What matters is the difference between what you actually paid and what you actually received.

There is also no need for a separate journal. A cash book is effectively two journals, and any adjustments can be made in the cash book, with a zero figure under 'bank'.

At the end of the year, the page columns are totalled and those totals are added to give the year-end figures, for your own satisfaction and for the taxman's interest.

3. Management Accounts

Management accounts are concerned with seeing *where* the money is earned; financial accounts are concerned just with recording how much was earned.

For investment management accounts, this means keeping track of how each share in your portfolio is doing. The first thing to do here is to keep track of what shares (and how many) are owned at any one time. If your portfolio is being managed, your broker will do this. Otherwise a simple ledger or equivalent should be sufficient.

Keep these records entirely separate from your financial accounting records.

Every time you sell a share, discipline yourself to calculate how much profit or loss you made overall. Include in this dividends received. Compare this with what you would have got had you put the money in a building society.

Remember to be perfectly objective and unemotional about what you have achieved. Neither gloat over your profits nor grieve over your losses. Just learn what lessons there are to learn.

4. Recording Moving Averages

In addition to keeping management accounts to determine how you *have* made a profit, you need records to help you *make* your profits.

The two easiest ways of doing this are to plot share prices on a graph and use the charting techniques explained in the previous chapter, or to use a system of moving averages, whose principles are also explained in the previous chapter.

Probably the simplest way of keeping a record is to enter a weekly (or possibly daily) record of share prices, using extra columns to calculate the moving average. If you decide to record weekly figures, choose a day and stick to it. Don't change the day one week because something has happened. The choice of day doesn't matter particularly, but Wednesday is often used as it is in the middle of the week and its prices may therefore reflect what has happened in the last week without being too influenced by suspicions about the following week. Also, Wednesdays tend to be boring and need something to liven them up.

Suppose you decide to use a five-week moving average and your share prices on consecutive Wednesdays are:

107 111 94 93 95 122 126 109 108 110 107 111

There is no need to take an average, a five-week total will do, as we are looking only for trends up and down. Dividing everything by five will not clarify things further.

So we can rule up our book with these headings and make entries as follows: '

Date	Share price	5-week total
31.12.8. .	107	
7.1.8. .	111	
14.1.8. .	94	
21.1.8. .	93	
28.1.8. .	95	500
4.2.8. .	122	515
11.2.8. .	126	530
18.2.8. .	109	545
25.2.8. .	108	560
4.3.8. .	110	575
11.3.8. .	107	560
18.3.8. .	111	545

To calculate the five-week total, you simply add the current week's share price to your previous total and subtract the figure for five weeks earlier. Five weeks is the shortest period for which it is worthwhile to record moving averages.

The result shows that the underlying trend is a simple peak, and therefore we sell on 11 March, when we first notice that the upward trend has reversed.

You will notice that we have no total for the first four weeks. We did not record their price as we weren't interested in the shares then. Those missing figures can always be found by looking up back copies of your newspaper.

5. Refinements to the System: Longer Averages

The above system is simple enough, but some accuracy has been sacrificed for the sake of simplicity.

To start with, a five-week average is short and only likely to detect short-term trends. It is often advisable, also, to calculate 13-week averages and 200-day averages.

In doing this two points must be stressed:

> i the average must be calculated, totals are not good enough,
>
> ii the average refers to a halfway point in time. Thus a 5-week average calculated up to 31 December gives you the average as at 2½ weeks earlier, i.e. 14 December; the 13-week average is for 6½ weeks earlier, i.e. 15 November; and the 200-day average is for 100 days earlier, i.e. 23 October. This means that

the different averages calculated on the same day must be entered against different dates on the table or graph.

So having plotted three different sets of moving averages, which one do we observe? The longer the average the clearer we can discern the trend, but the longer we have to wait before we can act on it. Clearly the question is a trade-off between accuracy and expediency.

In practice, the 13-week average tends to give the most often correct answers and send the fewest false alarms. If you are limited to calculating only one average, that is the one to use. However, the other averages should be consulted. The 200-day average could be regarded as a base line, and the 5-week average as indicating the short-term trend against that line.

If the 5-week average is moving ahead of the 13-week average which is moving ahead of the 200-day average, then buy. If the positions are reversed, sell.

If the 5-week average moves up but the 13-week average moves down, buy, but sell if the 5-week average turns down and the 13-week average carries on down. Hold the shares if the 13-week average turns up whatever the 5-week average does. The 200-day average can be used to verify the accuracy of the trend indicated by the 13-week average.

If the 13-week average moves up, hold the shares. Buy more when the 5-week average also moves up.

The above 'rules' are a little simplistic. With experience, you should be able to adapt them to your own portfolio. The speed with which you react to changes depends on whether you are a cautious or aggressive investor. The cautious investor pays more attention to the longer averages.

Do not forget to study the economy and how your company and its trade is doing within it. Also remember that there is nothing to stop you charting the shares as well.

6. Improving the System: Including General Measures

The above method will usually prove to be good enough in most practical applications. However, it ignores the effect of the economy as a whole. The result is that we can believe (particularly if we have a small portfolio) that a company is doing very well, when the truth is that its performance is relatively mediocre but the economy itself is booming.

Often this will not matter, but if we wish to refine our system further we can also plot a measure of the economy in the same way. The usual measure used is the FT 30-share index, but you may feel that another index is appropriate (see Chapter 6).

A further refinement is to divide the share price by the FT index. You can either divide the price by the index for that day or divide an average by the average index for the same period, the answers will be the same. The resultant number will not represent anything in itself, but its increase and decrease will show how the company is doing *relative to the rest of the economy*.

This figure is no alternative to the share's own moving average, but can alert you to a company or sector that is performing particularly well or particularly poorly.

If you are plotting values on a graph, a simple alternative is to plot the index on the same graph. If the shares are performing in line with the index, their lines will be parallel. Increases in the gap between them show that the company is doing better than the economy as a whole.

10. Tax

1. Introduction

There are five taxes that we need to consider:

    i Stamp duty
    ii Value added tax
    iii Income tax
    iv Capital gains tax
    v Inheritance tax.

Personal Equity Plans (see Chapter 11) were designed to encourage investment by granting relief from income tax and capital gains tax.

2. Stamp Duty

Stamp duty was first introduced in 1694 and is therefore the country's oldest tax (unless you include domestic rates first introduced in 1601).

Stamp duty is either a fixed amount (fixed duty) or is a percentage of some figure (*ad valorem* duty).

Unusually it is not a tax on actual transactions, but on the pieces of paper which give rise to the transaction. Generally, failure to pay stamp duty gives rise to no direct penalty (as it does for income tax), but makes the document invalid, usually invalidating the transaction. However, if you can legally make a transaction without the need for any documents, you can avoid stamp duty. For shares, an example would be a private agreement that shares held by one person are donated to a second, but held on trust for him by the first.

Extensive changes in stamp duty on share trading were made in the Finance Act 1985, with effect from the Big Bang (27 October 1986). From this date a new tax, stamp duty reserve tax was introduced.

Stamp duty is charged at 0.5 per cent, from 27 October 1986, before which it was 1 per cent. The value is the same as that used for capital gains tax purposes. In addition, a transfer stamp is payable. This is a fixed fee, often as small as 10p. These duties are calculated for you and shown on your contract note.

Also, from 27 October 1986:

i share exchanges during a transfer are exempt,
ii stamp duty reserve tax becomes payable on renounceable letters of allotment. This tax is administered differently from stamp duty, but the rate is the same, at 0.5 per cent.

3. Value Added Tax

Value added tax is charged at 15 per cent on the stockbroker's commission. Thus, if your stockbroker charges you 1 per cent, on a £1000 deal you will pay £10 commission plus £1.50 VAT.

Since the Big Bang there has been a curious exception that where a stockbroker uses his own market-maker, the whole transfer is exempt, with the result that no VAT is charged at all. The Stock Exchange wants this anomaly removed, but, apart from a technical measure relating to underwriting capital issues, the Chancellor did not do so in the March 1987 Budget.

VAT charged on commission is generally not reclaimable, even if you are registered for VAT. Input tax is only deductible if the supply is related to the company's business. This is not so for private investments.

4. Income Tax

Income tax is paid on the dividends you receive. It is not payable on any profit you make from selling the shares (except if your business is share-dealing). Income tax, however, is usually payable on the profits from dealing in traded options.

In practice, the amount of the dividend you receive has effectively already had basic rate tax deducted from it. Thus, if the tax rate is 27 per cent and you receive £146, you are regarded as having received £200 dividend on which you have already paid £54 income tax. This £54 is known as the 'tax credit'. The actual amount is shown on your dividend warrant. The same principle applies to bank and building society interest.

You are required to disclose the dividends you receive on your tax return, but you will not pay any more tax unless your total income makes you liable to the higher rates. The figure at which higher rate tax becomes payable is usually revised each year in the Budget.

If you are liable to tax at the higher rates, the *gross* figure is added to your other income, and the tax credit is deducted from your total tax liability. Thus, if you are liable to tax at the 45 per cent rate, your tax computation will include:

Dividend income	£200
Tax at 45%	£90
Less tax credit	£54
Additional tax payable	£36

You gross up the figure by multiplying the amount of money you actually received by:

$$\frac{100 - BR}{BR}$$

where BR is the basic rate of income tax.

Such additional tax is obtained by an assessment which covers other such assessable income.

The tax is payable in the tax year in which you actually received the dividend, not that to which the dividend relates. If no dividend is received, no tax is payable. There is therefore no equivalent of loss relief or bad debt relief for dividends.

An issue of shares in lieu of a dividend is treated as a dividend and is subject to income tax at an 'appropriate value'.

On the sale or purchase of shares, 'bondwashing' provisions may apply.

All dividend income is regarded as investment income for income tax purposes. Investment income was once subject to investment income surcharge. Although this was abolished in 1984, the distinction can still be important in other tax considerations (such as separate taxation of a wife's earnings, for example).

5. Capital Gains Tax

Capital gains tax is chargeable on your profits from buying and selling shares. It does not apply to the dividends you receive (these being subject to income tax). However it is unlikely that you will have to pay capital gains tax at all, as there is an annual exemption level below which it does not need to be paid (£6600 for 1987/88). Unless your total capital gains (from all sources, not just shares) exceed this figure, you will not be liable for the tax.

When shares are sold at a profit, the profit is subject to capital gains tax. Equally, when shares are sold at a loss, the loss may be offset against other profits and, if still not fully offset, may be stored indefinitely against future capital gains. Losses can also be offset against a capital gain on a husband's or wife's shares, provided that the couple were married and living together for the whole tax year (6 April to following 5 April).

Capital gains tax is charged at 30 per cent, but only after you exceed the exemption figure. The rate of tax has remained unchanged since the tax was introduced in 1965. The annual exemption is usually revised in the Budget.

Shares are valued using the 'quarter-up rule'. This is the buying price plus one quarter of the difference between the buying and selling prices. Thus, if a share is sold for 159p and bought for 151p, the 'quarter-up' figure is 153p.

Indexation was introduced in March 1982 to deal with objections that capital gains tax was a tax on inflation. If you had spent £313.40 on shares in March 1982 and sold them for £366.10 (after commissions, etc.) three years later, you would have made a profit of £52.70. However £366.10 in March 1985 was worth exactly the same as £313.40 in March 1982, so you would have made no profit in real terms, and it would be a bit unfair to pay tax on a 'profit' caused only by inflation. Indexation, therefore, allows you to reduce your profit figure by the amount that your original investment would have increased if affected by inflation alone It can reduce your profit to zero, turn a profit into a loss, or increase a loss. The index used is the Retail Price Index, though in practice Inland Revenue indexation tables are used.

There are very complex provisions regarding pooled assets, assets held before 31 March 1982, part disposals, rights issues, bonus issues, capital reorganisations and suchlike. These provisions are conveniently ignored in this book as they are unlikely to arise for the small investor.

6. Inheritance Tax

When you die, your shares are valued and included with the rest of your estate, which is subject to inheritance tax. Before 1986, this was known as capital transfer tax. An exception to this general rule is that inheritance tax is not payable on transfers to a surviving husband or wife.

There is an exemption up to which no tax is paid, (for example, £90,000 for 1987/88). The figure is usually revised each year in the Budget. Above this figure inheritance tax is paid at increasing rates from 30 to 60 per cent.

If property is given away in the seven years before death, it is also added back to the value of a person's estate, but is subject to taper relief.

People still talk about death duties, but these were abolished in 1974.

Finally, make sure that your next of kin know about your shareholdings. When a shareholder cannot be traced, the company pays the dividend into a special bank account and there it may well stay for ever. It is believed that these amounts now run into millions and, along with unclaimed bank balances, premium bonds, insurance claims, etc., could form a 'sleeping economy' of up to £1bn.

11. Personal Equity Plans

1. What are Personal Equity Plans?

Personal Equity Plans or PEPs were introduced from 1 January 1987 to encourage individuals to invest directly in the Stock Exchange. The encouragement comes in the form of tax relief. Your dividends are free of income tax and the profit on the sale of your shares is free of capital gains tax. As income tax has effectively been paid already on dividends, the plan manager reclaims that from the Revenue for you. It does not affect your liability to pay stamp duty, VAT and inheritance tax.

A PEP takes the form of a separate portfolio which must be managed by someone who has obtained Inland Revenue approval for the purpose. He is known as the plan manager. Each adult can invest up to £2400 per calendar year, either as a lump sum or as monthly payments. Some of this may be invested in unit trusts. This limit applies to each person, so a husband and wife can each have a plan. There is no minimum limit in the tax rules, but plan managers will usually want at least £360 a year invested.

Charges are made for running the service.

All the records are kept by the plan manager, so the PEP holder does not need to keep any records for tax purposes. However the PEP holder is the legal owner of all the shares in the portfolio, and he has all the legal rights of an ordinary shareholder, although it costs him more to exercise them.

2. The Rules

1 The shares must be in a separate portfolio, known as the equity plan.
2 The portfolio must be managed by an authorised plan manager.

3 The plan manager must keep proper records and make an annual return to the Inland Revenue.

4 The PEP holder must be at least 18 years old.

5 The PEP holder must be resident in the UK.

6 Subscriptions to the PEP must be made in cash. Existing shareholdings cannot be transferred into it.

7 The investment is limited to £2400 (plus any interest and dividends received) in any calendar year.

8 For a minimum period of one year, interest and dividends received must be 'rolled up', i.e. held or reinvested, not paid out in cash.

9 A person may have only one PEP. He cannot, for example, have two PEPs each for £1200. He can however change his PEP manager each calendar year.

10 Shares held must be ordinary shares of UK-incorporated companies listed on the UK Stock Exchange. Unit trusts must be authorised. Shares cannot be included for unlisted companies. Neither may a PEP invest in preference shares, debentures, fixed interest stock, options, futures, or gilts.

11 The holding in unit trusts is limited to the lower of 25 per cent of the investment and £420.

12 Partly paid shares are valued at the amount actually paid and are included for the years in which the payment is made.

13 The amount of the plan which may be held in cash is limited to the greater of 10 per cent of the plan and £240.

14 All dealings must be at open market price. Trading on margin and going 'short' are not allowed.

15 The investments must be held for at least one year before being sold. If the proceeds of any sale are reinvested within 28 days, the reinvestment does not count as part of that year's investment limit, and the sale proceeds are free of capital gains tax. The reinvestment must be made in qualifying securities.

16 The PEP holder can withdraw his money at any time, but if the minimum conditions have not been met, the tax reliefs are lost.

17 The PEP holder must always have the opportunity to exercise shareholder's rights.

For a list of plan managers whose PEP schemes have been approved by the Inland Revenue see Appendix B.

12. Quick Guide to Company Law

1. Limited Liability

A limited company is a registered body whose liability to any third party is limited to what the body itself can provide. The members (shareholders) of a limited company (unlike members of a partnership) have no liability, except to pay the nominal value of their shares.

A limited company can either be private or public. A public company is one where the public can buy and sell its shares. Public companies have 'plc' (public limited company) after their name. Private companies have 'Ltd' (limited).

Public companies are either 'listed' or 'unlisted'. A listed company is one which is listed on the Stock Exchange. Sometimes 'quoted' is used instead of 'listed'.

Every company has a memorandum of association and articles of association. These are the terms of what is effectively a legally binding contract between the members, and between the members and the company. Any member is entitled to have a copy on payment of a nominal fee (though few ever exercise this right).

These documents are usually fairly short and uninformative. The longest section states the objects of the company. This is a totally pointless relic of a bygone age, as most are written so that the company can do what it likes anyway. It was designed to stop people raising money 'for carrying on an undertaking of great advantage but nobody to know what it is', as someone (very successfully) did in 1720. He disposed of 1000 shares in six hours. History fails to record what the great advantage was (probably none).

The care and control of the company is vested in the directors alone. The shareholders' rights are confined to appointing the directors and asking them awkward questions at the annual general meeting.

Every company must have a registered office and a company secretary (who may also be a director). The company secretary is responsible for making sure that the company meets its legal requirements. If you need to communicate with the company as a shareholder, you should write to the company secretary at the registered office.

A limited company effectively borrows money from its shareholders (and sometimes others) with which it trades to make a profit. Corporation tax is payable on the profits. The rest is either kept by the company (retained profit) or distributed as a dividend.

Money borrowed may take the form of a saleable instrument (e.g. share, debenture, loan stock, etc.). These are explained further below. Other types of investment are explained in Chapter 13.

2. Types of Share

Your rights as a shareholder depend on the type of shares you own. Generally we have assumed throughout this book that you own ordinary voting shares, but there are many other types.

Ordinary voting shares entitle you to receive dividends and to vote according to the size of your shareholding. Ordinary shares are sometimes called 'equities' and ordinary share capital is sometimes called 'equity' or 'equity capital'.

Sometimes shares are called 'A' or 'B' shares. These are shares with different voting arrangements. Usually 'A' shares have no votes at all, but this is not always so.

Loan stock takes many forms, most of which can be traded just like shares, but which have a quite different legal status. Holders of loan stock do not own the company, they have simply lent money to the company.

The commonest form of loan stock is the debenture. This will be indicated with a percentage, e.g. '8% debenture'. This means that the holder receives a fixed return (in this case 8 per cent) *regardless of the profits of the company*. If he has £100 in 8 per cent debentures, he will receives £8 a year regardless of what profits have been made.

Debentures sometimes appear with a date, e.g. '8% debenture 1990/91'. This means that the debenture is redeemable, i.e. in 1990/91 the company can redeem the share by repaying the sum you originally lent. Sometimes the company *must* redeem the debentures then, sometimes it *may* redeem them. Sometimes only some debentures are redeemed. This is usually done by lot, and the redeemed debenture numbers are printed, like bingo numbers, in advertisements in the financial press.

Debentures are issued according to a deed. This sets out the debenture holders' rights, which usually include the provision to appoint a receiver if the debenture holders' rights are put in jeopardy.

Preference shares are a hybrid between the ordinary share and debenture. They are similar to debentures in that they carry an interest rate, but differ in the rights given to the holders. The interest on preference shares, like debentures, must be paid out of profits before the ordinary shareholders are paid.

Preference shares can variously be described as 'cumulative', 'participating' and 'convertible'.

'Cumulative' means that if the dividend (at the fixed rate) is not paid one year because the profits are too low, it is rolled over and becomes payable when the profits are sufficient. If the preference share is non-cumulative, unpaid dividends are lost for good.

'Participating' means that, in addition to receiving your fixed interest return, you can also participate in the profits of the company by a dividend in a way similar to ordinary shareholders.

Sometimes they are called 'convertible'. This means they may be converted to ordinary shares. This can be at the company's discretion or the preference shareholder's discretion or at neither's discretion. It can be at a fixed date, or at no fixed date, or within a specified period. It all depends on the terms of their issue.

Conversion of preference shares obviously increases the number of ordinary shares and therefore reduces the earning per (ordinary) share (eps). This is known as 'dilution'. Sometimes the eps and other figures are calculated according to the number of ordinary shares that would be in existence if all the convertible preference shares were converted.

For example, let us imagine that a company has 500 £1 ordinary shares, and 200 £1 8 per cent preference shares which can be converted to ordinary shares at a 2-to-1 ratio. The company makes a profit of £2400. Its eps is therefore 480p

(£2400 ÷ 500). But if the preference shares are converted to ordinary shares, there will be an extra 100 ordinary shares, so the diluted eps is only 400p (£2400 ÷ 600).

'Deferred' shares are ordinary shares whose right to a dividend ranks after other ordinary shares. These are sometimes called founders' shares as they were often issued to the people who started the business initially.

'Partly-paid' shares are shares whose nominal value (see next section) has not been fully paid. British Gas shares, for example, had a nominal value of 130p, but were paid in three stages (known as 'calls') of 40p, 40p and 50p. When the last 50p per share was paid, the shares were 'fully paid'; until then they were partly paid. If you fail to pay a call on partly-paid shares, you lose the shares completely. This is known as 'forfeiture'.

The law generally requires partly-paid shares to be issued for at least 25 per cent of their par value plus premium.

'Labour shares' are ordinary or preference shares reserved for the workforce under an employee share scheme. For UK companies they have the same rights as other ordinary or preference shares, but for Australian and New Zealand companies they sometimes have restrictions on the right to transfer.

3. Par Value

All shares of UK companies must have a 'par value', also known as the 'nominal value'. This is the amount that the shareholder *originally* subscribed (i.e. paid) for the share.

If a company is profitable its shares will soon be worth more than the amount originally subscribed, and this is why shares are usually sold for much more than their par value. However, you cannot measure how well a company is doing simply by dividing its share price by the nominal value. You do not know how long the company has been in existence and how long, therefore, it has taken to build up that value. Similarly you do not know how many rights and bonus issues there have been which would further help to distort such comparison.

The only *duty* of a shareholder is to pay the par value of the share when called upon to do so. Unless the share is partly-paid, this will have been done when the share was bought. Unlike a member of a partnership, the shareholder cannot be made to cough up any more money if the company goes into insolvent liquidation.

As nominal values are fairly meaningless, the USA and Canada allow shares to be issued at no par value (sometimes abbreviated 'npv'). Such practice is illegal in the UK but overseas npv may legally be traded in the UK. Attempts have been made at various times (the last in 1967) to allow npv shares in the UK, but the idea has always been turned down.

The par value and voting rights determine the 'class' of the share. If two shares have the same value and voting rights, they are said to be of the same class.

Sometimes a company may wish to issue more shares of the same class as shares already in issue. Suppose that these shares were ordinary 25p voting shares which currently enjoy a market value of 60p. Clearly the company will not wish to sell these new shares for only 25p, so the law allows it to sell them at a price above the par value. The amount of the excess (35p a share in this case) does not become part of the company's ordinary share capital but is shown separately as a share premium account. There are strict rules about what may be done with a share premium account, and also when shares may be issued *below* the par value.

4. Types of Share Issue

There are four main types of share issue:

    i Equity issue (or 'public issue'),
   ii Bonus issue (or 'scrip issue'),
  iii Capitalisation issue, and
  iv Rights issue.

An *equity issue* is a sale of completely new shares, regardless of what shares may already have been issued and who holds them. Such an issue is made by an issuing house, often a merchant bank. The issue is usually underwritten which means that the underwriter agrees to buy any shares which remain unsold. Sales of such shares are made against a prospectus telling potential investors about the company. The prospectus must comply with strict rules laid down in law and by the Stock Exchange.

A *bonus issue* is where extra shares are given to existing shareholdings in proportion to their holdings. It is a mistake to think that you are being given something for nothing; you still own exactly the same amount of the company as you did before. Typically, you may own 100 £1 shares which the company, by a bonus issue, turns into 400 25p shares. It is a book-keeping exercise only. A common reason for a bonus issue is to split up shares that have acquired a high unit price so as to make them more marketable.

A *capitalisation issue* is similar to a bonus issue, but here you are getting something extra. The company is effectively turning its retained profit into extra shares and distributing them in proportion to the shareholders' existing holdings. Again, you still own the same proportion of the company, and the company has become no more or less profitable. You may find, though, that your dividends increase in total amount as a result.

A *rights issue* is a combination of an equity issue and bonus issue. The company is selling more shares, but offers them first to existing shareholders in proportion to their holdings. Thus, if you own 500 shares and the company makes a 1 for 4 rights issue, you will be invited to subscribe for another 125 shares. The price you are asked to pay will be less than the current market value.

Clearly if all the shareholders exercise their right to buy, the relative size of their shareholdings will remain unchanged. However, you may not wish to invest money in that company, or you may not be able to afford to do so, so you decline to accept the offer and your shareholding reduces in relative size. However, as the shares have provisionally been allocated to you at less than the market price, the provisional letter of allotment itself is worth something, and you can sell the letter and the rights for a sum slightly less than the difference between the offer price of the shares and their market value.

5. Stages in Issuing Shares

A public company must have a minimum share capital of £50,000, but most have a far larger sum.

The maximum amount is given in the company's memorandum of association and is known as the 'authorised share capital'.

The amount of share capital which has actually been issued is known as the 'issued share capital'. Often these amounts are the same, but the issued share capital can be less.

The amount of par value which has actually been paid is known as the 'paid-up share capital'. If there are no partly-paid shares in issue, the paid-up share capital is the same as the issued share capital.

The process by which shares are issued is known as subscription. The investor 'applies' for shares at an advertised price. (Sales by tender are discussed below.) It would be a remarkable coincidence if the applications exactly matched the shares available, so an issue is said to be either oversubscribed or undersubscribed.

If undersubscribed, the underwriters purchase the unsold shares. If no underwriting arrangement has been made, or the arrangement is insufficient, the issue has failed and the shares may not be legally issued.

If oversubscribed, the company either holds a ballot or gives the investors a portion of what they asked for, or both. The issue of TSB shares was so heavily oversubscribed that they had to do both. It should be stated that there is much tactical application in issues which are expected to be oversubscribed. For example, if you want 500 shares in X plc but you think it might be oversubscribed five times, you can apply for 2500 shares in the hope of getting the 500 you want. The risk is that you will be allocated more than 500 which you may not be able to accept and consequently lose your right to buy the shares at all. The fact that a share issue is oversubscribed 27 times (as Thames Television was) does not necessarily mean that investors wanted 27 times as many shares as were available!

Sometimes shares are offered 'for tender'. This means that as well as saying how many shares you want, you also say how much you are prepared to pay. Assuming that the issue is oversubscribed, the issuing house then finds the price at which, and above which, enough investors have tendered for all the shares to be issued. This is known as the 'striking price' and is paid by all investors, even though they may have tendered a higher figure. Those who tendered a lower figure receive nothing. Virgin was successfully floated by a tender offer.

The process by which shares are matched to investors is called *allotment*. You receive a letter of allotment, telling you how many shares have been allotted to you and how much you have to pay.

The letter of allotment will be either 'renounceable' or 'provisional'. If it is renounceable (as is usual for rights issues), you have a short time (often six weeks) in which you may sell your letter of allotment. If you neither take up your allotment nor sell your right to do so, the allotment lapses. A provisional allotment may either be accepted or rejected within the stated time limit. It cannot be sold.

You become the legal owner of the shares when you take up your allotment. The share certificate may take a little while to be prepared and sent to you.

From any time when you become the legal owner you can sell them, even if you have not received the share certificate.

Even before the shares have been allotted to you it is possible to sell shares on what is known as the 'grey market'. This is very risky, however, because if you have sold shares which are not allocated to you, you can be forced to buy the shares on the open market, probably at a substantial loss.

6. Transfer and Registration

The share certificate is your proof that you own the shares, though all is not lost if the certificate is lost or destroyed. In some circumstances the certificate is regarded as prima facie evidence of title, but the difference is a fine legal point.

One of your rights as a shareholder is that you can transfer your shares to whom you like when you like. A public company cannot restrict your right to sell your shares.

When a shareholder dies, his shares are said to be *transmitted* rather than transferred, though the procedure is similar.

The company records you as a shareholder in its register of members when you have taken up an allotment or had shares transferred or transmitted to you. It must issue a share certificate within two months. The share certificate will usually be numbered, though this is not a legal requirement.

The register of members is usually kept at the company's registered office. A copy of it is sent every year with the company's annual return to the Registrar of Companies. The register is open to inspection by anyone.

7. Shareholders' Rights

A shareholder has many rights, though in public companies these are more apparent than real.

For the record, the shareholder has the right to:

    i be paid a dividend if profits allow. In practice the directors announce the dividend and the shareholders meekly accept;

    ii receive a copy of the annual accounts and reports. Companies are required by Stock Exchange rules to send out a half-year summary also. Often companies prepare quarterly accounts which are available to shareholders on request;

    iii appoint the directors;

    iv appoint the auditors. The auditors are answerable only to the shareholders, though in practice all the shareholders get (for what is often a six-figure sum) is a maximum of 100 words, and even they are copied out of an Institute of Chartered Accountants leaflet. The only people who get any real information are the directors, who are the very people the auditors are supposed to be checking on!

    v attend general meetings. The company must have an annual general meeting every calendar year within 15 months of the previous meeting. Further meetings are called extraordinary general meetings;

    vi vote on all resolutions (assuming the shares carry a vote). Some resolutions require more than a 50 per cent vote. A shareholder who cannot attend a meeting may vote by proxy;

    vii question the directors at a general meeting. In practice little time is provided for this and a shareholder can easily be denied this right;

    viii inspect the register of members without charge;

    ix be provided with a copy of the memorandum and articles of association of the company (on payment of a modest fee).

There are additional remedies for shareholders to protect them from abuse by directors and majority shareholders. There are also rights in connection with liquidations and in convening extraordinary general meetings.

8. Shareholders' Perks

Some companies offer discounts or free gifts to shareholders. These are usually nominal in value. Shares should not be bought just for the perks, though the perks could tip the balance in the company's favour.

The following companies are known to offer discounts or gifts provided there is a minimum shareholding:

Alexander Holdings (Ford cars)
Allied–Lyons (meals, hotels)
Arenson Group (furniture)
Associated British Food (grocery)
Austin Reed (shoes, sports gear)
BSG International (cars)
Barclays Unicorn (cruises)
Barr and Wallace Arnold Trust (cars, package holidays)
Barratt Developments (houses)
Bass (holidays, hotels)
Bellway (kitchen units, new house)
Bentalls (products sold, hairdressing)
Boots (own brand products)
Burton Group (carpet, clothing)
Courts (furniture)
Eldridge Pope (alcoholic drink)
Emess Lighting (light fittings)
Cecil Gee (clothing)
Gieves Group (clothing)
Grand Metropolitan Hotels (drinks, holidays, meals)
Greenall Whitley (hotels)
Hawley Group (discount on Alpine double glazing,
　　Dolphin showers, Sharps furniture)
Hillards (products sold in stores)
Horizon Travel (holidays)
Imperial Group (Breakaway weekend for two)
John Kent (clothing)
Kwik-Fit (car tyres and exhausts)
LWT Holdings (holidays)
Ladbroke Group (hotels, restaurants)
Lonrho (Volkswagen and Audi cars, hotels, holidays, car
　　services, jewellery, Brentford textiles)
Manders Holdings (brushes, wallpaper, paint, etc.)

Mellaware International (kitchen utensils)
Milletts Leisure Shops (camping equipment, clothing)
Moss Bros (clothing)
Next (clothing)
Norfolk Capital (hotels, restaurants)
P & O (travel)
Pentos (furniture and books)
Peters Stores (camping equipment, clothing)
Prince of Wales Hotels (holidays)
Alfred Preedy (food)
Rank Organisation (holidays)
Riley Leisure (snooker tables and cues)
Rover Group (cars)
Scottish and Newcastle Breweries (hotels)
Sharpe and Fisher (DIY and gardening items)
Sketchley (dry cleaning)
Spear and Jackson (gardening tools and lawnmowers)
Stylo (shoes)
Toye and Co. (regalia, trophies, etc.)
Trafalgar House (cruises, hotels)
Trusthouse Forte (hotels)
E. Upton and Sons (discount on goods sold at stores)
Vaux Group (hotels, meals)
Whitbread (various).

Fuller details are given in the third edition of *Shareholders Perks* by Blackstone Franks, published by Kogan Page Ltd, 120 Pentonville Road, London N1 9JN: 01–278 0433.

9. Takeovers

If another company decides to take over the company whose shares you own, you will be wooed to sell your shares.

The company being taken over is called the 'target company', and the company seeking to take it over is called a 'predator'.

A takeover is either friendly (the target company agrees) or hostile (the target company does not agree). Sometimes more than one predator may be trying, which is known as a contested takeover bid.

The usual reason for a takeover is that the target company is seen as not fully using its potential. The management is seen as poor.

You will either be offered cash for your shares, or shares in the predator company in exchange, or both. Sometimes you are given a choice.

If the takeover is contested, you will be bombarded with leaflets and brochures telling you why you should/should not accept the offer because the predator company is/is not better equipped to run the target company. There will often be advertisements in the financial press and plenty of news coverage.

Many of these brochures are works of literature in the way in which they use the same facts to produce opposite conclusions.

Human ingenuity is rarely so thoroughly exercised as when defending a takeover bid. The many defences are known by colourful names such as: white knight, Pac-man strategy, shark repellant, poison pills, crown jewels, sandbag, Lady Macbeth strategy, etc. These are explained in the glossary.

A takeover usually pushes up the price of the target company's shares markedly, and may also increase the predator's share price.

It is rare that the private investors' decisions make much difference to the outcome (the famous fight over Westland Helicopters was an exception). The private investor is usually best advised to wait until the last minute (by which time the original offer is likely to have improved) and go with the crowd. And enjoy the fun!

13. Other Types of Investment

1. Unit Trusts

A unit trust is effectively a ready-made portfolio to which the investor subscribes by buying units. The investor is known as the unitholder. His rights end with the unit trust; he has no equity in the shares it holds. These are held by trustees on behalf of the trust.

Most unit trusts are 'open-ended'. That means that they guarantee to buy back units when you want.

Unit trusts are effectively a halfway house between deposit accounts and shares. It can be the ideal medium for someone who wants to invest in the Stock Exchange, but has insufficient capital to do so.

Unit trusts are also safer. They sometimes do lose value, but never to zero.

The values of units in unit trusts are printed in the financial press with share prices.

2. Gilts

Gilts, or gilt-edged securities, are government-backed securities. They are so named because the certificates originally had gilt edges.

The government does not trade, but repays the investor from state income, including taxes. Money lent in gilts is used to fund the Public Sector Borrowing Requirement (PSBR).

No government has ever yet defaulted on a gilt-edged security, and there seems little chance at present that any government ever will. They are therefore considered very safe, and are often included in portfolios which need such safety.

Gilts are issued for repayment of a fixed amount at a set date. Tenders are invited for amounts less than the fixed repayment, the difference representing the effective investment income. Once issued, the gilts are traded like shares and other securities.

If the gilt is for less than five years, it is called 'short-dated'. Short-dated gilts are sometimes just called 'shorts'. Between five and ten years, they are called medium-dated. For more than ten years, they are called long-dated.

Sometimes the government issues securities with no fixed repayment date. The best-known is consolidated stock, more commonly known as 'consols'. These were first issued in the eighteenth century and take their name from the fact that they consolidated the national debt. They carry interest at 2½ per cent per annum and sell at a price which reflects the yield on comparable securities.

Local authorities and the governments of other countries also issue securities, usually on a similar basis to the British government.

3. Traded Options

Traded options are a suitable investment medium only for those who know what they are doing.

You do not buy or sell shares at all, but buy or sell *the right* to buy or sell shares at a fixed price in the future. The option period is fixed. Three periods are quoted per share, of three, six and nine months. When the first three-month period has expired, making the six- and nine-month options in three- and six-month options respectively, a new nine-month option is launched. The option to buy the shares can be taken at any time within the option period. Alternatively the option itself can be sold. If neither happens within the period, the option is lost – and so is the option money.

There are three types of option: 'call', 'put' and 'double'. A call option is the right to buy, a put option is the right to sell, a double option is the right to do either. The fee for an option (the 'option money') is usually in the order of 10 to 15 per cent of the share price. Options are usually sold for units of 1000 shares.

An option allows the investor to make a much higher return on his investment. Whereas good share dealing could make 50 per cent, good option dealing can make several hundred per cent. The downside is that you can just as quickly lose the lot. Also you cannot hold on to them while you wait for the price to recover.

An advantage is that by being such high-risk investments, they can be used to increase the risk factor in a portfolio. Options can, however, also be used to reduce a risk. For example, if we buy shares expecting them to rise in value, we can protect the risk of their falling by buying a put option for the same shares.

The traded options market started in London in 1978, and has proved very popular. In January 1987 the daily average of contracts was 43,086, compared with 14,571 just one year earlier. Growth is currently in the order of 6 to 7 per cent a month, meaning that the volume of business doubles every eight months.

The options market has also provided a useful means of measuring how share prices are expected to move. The market (at 28 February 1987) was limited to just 45 equity shares (including all the components of the FT 30-share index), one long-term and one short-term gilt, two exchange rates (dollar/sterling and DM/sterling) and the FT–SE 100 index.

Unlike share dealing, option dealing is regarded as trading and may be taxed as such under Schedule D Case I or VI. Where shares are actually bought or sold, the cost of the option may be allowed in determining any capital gain.

Traded option deals are transacted by stockbrokers as for shares.

4. Other Markets

Most UK share dealing is done on the London Stock Exchange. There are, however, also recognised stock exchanges in Belfast, Birmingham, Bristol, Dublin, Glasgow, Leeds, Liverpool, Manchester and Newcastle. The regional exchanges operate on similar lines to the London exchange. (Together they all form the International Stock Exchange of the UK and the Republic of Ireland.)

Also, as an alternative to a full Stock Exchange listing, a company's shares may be traded on:

     i the Unlisted Securities Market (USM),
     ii the Third Tier market, or
     iii the Over-the-Counter Market (OTC).

Trading in the first two markets is done in the usual way by stockbrokers. They exist to provide an exchange for companies for whom a full listing is not appropriate.

These markets are not physical locations, but areas of trade. The first two operate as for other shares traded on the London Stock Exchange.

The *Unlisted Securities Market* was established in November 1980 and deals in gamma shares. Such companies are said to be 'admitted' to the USM, not listed on it. They must comply with the less onerous regulations found in what is known as the 'Green Book'.

The USM started with eleven companies and now deals in over 500.

In addition, specific bargains in companies which are neither listed nor admitted, and deals in some otherwise ineligible mineral exploration companies may be transacted in what are known respectively as section 535.2 and 535.3 deals. The names come from the authorising sections of the Stock Exchange rulebook. USM companies tend to be respectable but small, with a higher risk than listed companies.

It was expected that the Big Bang would adversely affect the USM. In fact the opposite happened. USM business rose by 35 per cent in the first eight weeks after the Big Bang. Over £1bn worth of business is now transacted daily on the USM.

The *Third Market* came into being on 26 January 1987 for companies for whom even the USM conditions are too onerous. The Stock Exchange describes these as 'young growth companies'. Eight companies were traded on this market on its first day, and another 62 were said to be preparing for admission. The shares are either gamma or (if less than two market dealers deal in them) delta. Companies are bound by some simple Stock Exchange rules.

It is too early to comment on its success or otherwise, but feelings generally seem to be optimistic.

The *Over-the-Counter Market* is effectively a bucket shop. Unlike the other two markets, it is not governed by the Stock Exchange. OTC deals may be in any share. The OTC market has persistently been outperformed by the other markets.

5. Overseas Shares

As part of diversifying your portfolio, do not ignore the possibilities of shares in overseas companies. When the UK market is unsettled, e.g. just before a general election or during a bear period, it is often advisable to invest quite heavily overseas. Even during settled periods, there are good reasons to diversify overseas. In early 1987 some stockbrokers were recommending that up to 15 per cent of a small investor's portfolio should be in overseas companies.

Until 1979 there were restrictions on such investments under the Exchange Control Act 1947. The Act was repealed in 1987. It was previously suspended for general effect in 1979, but given limited reinstatement against Argentina during the Falklands War of 1982.

Some overseas securities are quoted on the London Stock Exchange, but there is nothing to stop you dealing on a foreign stock exchange.

The main factors to remember with overseas shares are:

   i commissions can be higher (typically up to 2 per cent),
   ii there is less access to information on which to make investment decisions, and
   iii the companies are subject to different laws and rules,
   iv tax becomes more complicated.

As regards tax, many overseas dividends will be subject to withholding tax in the overseas country. There are double taxation treaties whose provisions generally limit your total tax liability to the higher rate of the two countries. Sometimes tax can be saved by channelling dividends through third countries.

The accountants Touche Ross have developed a computer program, unfortunately only available to their own staff, which will work out tax-effective routes for you. The Netherlands Antilles is a particularly popular route. The firm will advise you on investments on a 'one-off' basis, but it is generally advisable to ask the firm to handle your entire overseas portfolio for you.

As a final practical point, lost overseas share certificates can be very expensive to replace.

6. Property

If you want capital growth and no income at all, property of various types provides the ideal investment.

Property can be in gold and jewellery, fine art, land and buildings, collectors' pieces, wine, and anything else that may appreciate in value with age.

However it should be remembered that many of these items have very limited markets, and the saleable value (particularly of lower value collectors' pieces) will only be a small fraction of the price quoted in catalogues.

Similarly, jewellery has little value above the value of the metal and stones used in it, unless the piece is of exceptional craftmanship. Your wedding ring and other domestic jewellery is not an investment. Its saleable value will rarely be more than half what you paid for it.

To invest in fine art requires a specialist's skill. The auction houses offer a comprehensive valuation service and produce indices of how prices have moved for particular categories of fine art.

Land and buildings provide the safest security of all, but again specialist knowledge is needed. There are moves to allow shares to be sold for specific properties, so you could, for example, own 2 per cent of an office block. This is likely to happen in the next few years, but in the meantime the objective can be achieved by buying shares in a property company.

It is possible to buy shares in a British ship. There are often 64 shares to a ship.

If investing in property, remember that your capital growth must also cover the expenses of insuring the property and, probably, such things as storage, valuation, etc.

7. Venture Capital

Venture capital is an investment in a company on a much larger scale. The venture capitalist often provides most if not all of the initial capital and often becomes more closely involved in the management of the business.

Unlike other share dealing discussed in this book, there is no need for the company to be a public company.

Venture capital should be seen as a halfway house between investment and running your own business. Such arrangements are usually made as a result of a newspaper advertisement or by using an accountant (often from one of the larger firms) as an intermediary. Venture capital deals are often made under the aegis of the Business Expansion Scheme which allows generous tax concessions.

Venture capitalism has spawned its own colourful vocabulary which the investment group calls 'venturespeak'. Some of the more relevant terms are given in the glossary.

Venture capital should be seen as a high-risk long-term venture, usually requiring much larger sums than for normal portfolio investment.

14. Other Things You Might Ask

1. What Was the Big Bang?

The Big Bang is a package of reforms introduced in the Stock Exchange on 27 October 1987.

It was designed to deal with two quite separate problems. One was an investigation by the Department of Trade and Industry into its restrictive practices. The other was the need to become part of a worldwide 24-hour market. This meant that London, Tokyo and New York each open for eight hours a day, and the London exchange had to invest in new computerised dealing equipment to catch up with the other two markets.

The occasion was also used to make other changes. Stockjobbers became market-makers. Fixed commissions were abolished. Stamp duty was cut from 1 to 0.5 per cent, but was extended in scope.

The term 'Big Bang' was first used by the chairman of the Stock Exchange to emphasise that changes were not to be made piecemeal. (The term originally referred to a theory of the creation of the universe.)

2. What Is Insider Dealing?

Insider dealing is profitable share dealing using information not generally known and gained from being in a privileged position (e.g. a director or auditor).

This is a criminal offence, first made illegal in the Companies Act 1980 (now consolidated in the Companies Act 1985).

In the following years there were very few prosecutions for insider dealings, even though many share prices mysteriously moved just before big news broke about that company. The obvious conclusion was that insider dealing was still rife.

In 1987 Geoffrey Collier became the first person to be convicted of insider dealing. He received a suspended prison sentence, but the real punishment was the loss of his job, the probable loss of his career and the public humiliation which he suffered as a result.

A more vigorous attack has now been made by the Financial Services Act 1986. There is now a Securities and Investments Board (SIB) whose functions include looking out for insider deals. There is also now a treaty with the US equivalent, the Securities Exchange Commission (SEC). By the end of 1986 there were serious charges of insider dealing outstanding against many previously highly regarded dealers.

A similar illegal practice is 'warehousing'. It is generally illegal for a company to buy its own shares or provide financial help for someone else to. A warehousing arrangement is where shares are bought up by a friendly third party prior to, say, a takeover bid in which the bidder's shares are part of the takeover consideration. The warehousing company then sells these shares back, usually at a guaranteed price, and is paid a fee. This was the main accusation outstanding against Guinness in 1987.

Other doubtful (though not necessarily illegal) City practices will be found listed in the glossary under the headings: concert party, dawn raid and grey knight. The list is not exhaustive.

3. Isn't It All Just a Gamble?

It can be, but this is really an abuse of the system rather than a proper use of it.

Trading is the whole basis of our civilisation. Without it, we would quickly return to being a primitive society. A prerequisite of all trade is the capital with which to trade. Companies can only raise this capital in a practical way if those who provide it can freely trade their investments. The Stock Exchange provides this service.

It is only by such means that banks, building societies, pension funds, insurance companies, etc., can earn the income with which to meet their commitments.

There can also be few objections on religious grounds. The Old Testament law did not prohibit interest payments on commercial deals, but did on loans to relieve poverty. In the New Testament, the parable of the talents (Matthew 25:14–30) specifically commends earning income from investments. The Church of England currently derives 42 per cent of its income from investments. Islamic law is stricter, but the problems have not proved insuperable.

Share prices provide a very quick and flexible measure of how a company is doing. This, in turn, provides a stimulus for the company to do well, which ultimately benefits the whole economy.

4. Don't the Stock Exchange Computers Keep Breaking Down?

No. There were some problems immediately after the Big Bang, but they were not as serious as was made out.

Basically the Stock Exchange uses two computer systems: SEAQ and TOPIC. SEAQ is used to make the transactions, TOPIC records information about deals and prices. When this new system was launched, many stockbrokers, fascinated with their new toy, overloaded TOPIC with the inevitable results.

5. Aren't the Stockbrokers the Only Winners?

No. It cannot be denied that many stockbrokers are very wealthy, but they have achieved this wealth by investing wisely themselves or by earning lots of commission by investing wisely for clients.

If a stockbroker's judgement is good enough for himself, it should be good enough for you. Similarly if he can become so rich on his 1.65 per cent commission, think what you can do on your share of the other 98.35 per cent!

6. Could the Wall Street Crash Happen Again?

It has, but the consequences will probably prove less devastating (see Chapter 15).

The Wall Street crash of 1929 occurred because prices had been hyped up to way above their intrinsic values. When the bubble burst, share prices plunged down, creating a downward momentum which pushed them further down. Many small investors had borrowed money to buy shares and were unable to meet the loan repayments. Investors and stockbrokers both chose to ignore that manufacturing was actually in decline. These factors led to the great depression from 1929 to 1935.

Before October 1987, the second largest 'crash' on Wall Street occurred on 11 September 1986 when the Dow–Jones index fell 86.61 points in one day. The world barely noticed.

7. Aren't Stockbrokers Snowed Under with Uncleared Paperwork?

It depends when you are reading this book!

By August 1987 the volume of share dealing was three times that of nine months earlier. Stockbrokers and market-makers were simply not geared up to handle this sort of increase in work. The problem was exacerbated by large privatisation issues, particularly Rolls-Royce. Many stockbrokers refused to deal with BAA shares a few months later.

At this time, it was also reported that paperwork had not been completed on some transactions six months old. Even the Bank of England began to put pressure on the Stock Exchange to clear the backlog.

The Stock Exchange responded by introducing two new rules. One allowed the Stock Exchange to impose fines on stockbroking firms which fail to settle bargains 'in a timely and efficient manner'. The other allows the Stock Exchange's own Council to initiate the purchase of shares and deliver the share certificates and to charge the cost to the delinquent firm.

Efforts have also been made to speed up the process of registering share certificates. The promised TAURUS computer system will also greatly ease the problem.

The main problem is that stockbrokers have simply been too greedy and taken on more work than they can properly perform before the systems could handle it.

8. Do Stockbrokers Give a Good Service to Individual Shareholders?

Again, it depends when you are reading this book.

As the volume of work trebled after the Big Bang, and the backlog built up, it was inevitable that stockbrokers would seek to look after the bigger more important customers at the expense of the little ones.

By August 1987, many of the 'no frills' share-dealing services had been discontinued or suspended, and there were many complaints that stockbrokers refused to answer the telephone.

The first substantial fall in the Stock Exchange since the Big Bang occurred on 5 and 6 August 1987, when the FT Ordinary Share index fell 50 points and some shares lost 25 per cent of their value. The 'small bargains' counter was closed completely, and small investors were left powerless to deal at all.

Many investors using stockbrokers and banks have also found that shares have been transacted at prices much worse than those that prevailed when the instructions were given.

The author's view is that this poor service cannot continue. It must be worth someone's while to provide a good service to a market of 8½ million customers. The banks and the new style of share shops being pioneered by people like Debenhams may provide some of the answer.

9. What Does the Stock Exchange Do for Small Investors?

It has set up a club for small investors designed to remove the mystique of share ownership. Membership costs £15 a year. Members receive a quarterly newsletter.

10. What About Investment Companies?

There are good and bad companies. Hopefully the latter will be thinned out when the Financial Services Act becomes fully effective.

Until then, investors have little protection when things go wrong. When the Charney Davies Group (thirteen companies) crashed in 1987, many of its 4,000 investors found they had lost all their savings and were unlikely to receive any compensation, despite the group's membership of FIMBRA.

In contrast, when the stockbroking firm of Giles & Overbury was 'hammered' (i.e. declared insolvent) in 1987, investors were fully protected. Giles & Overbury were the first stockbrokers to be hammered since 1984.

Harvard Securities has had a running battle with the Stock Exchange for at least ten years. Its latest application to the Stock Exchange, in July 1987, was rejected on the grounds that it was not a fit and proper firm. No specific charge of misconduct was made against the firm but many investors had complained about it.

11. What Do I Do about the Junk Mail I Get from Finance Companies?

Read it or bin it. They may have got your name and address when you filled in a card or from a ready-made list sold by a marketing agency. It is possible for you to be on more than one such list and therefore to get two or more copies of the same leaflet (the author's record is seven). Don't write to point this out. It is cheaper for them to send you two copies than to alter their computer.

If you want to cut down on junk mail, you can write to Mailing Preference Service, Freepost 22, London W1E 7EZ, who will circulate your name and address to its members.

Holding shares may in itself put you on such a mailing list. There was controversy when the Conservative party used British Telecom's shareholder list for a mail shot, but it is hard to see the objection. We live in a free country where you may write to whom you wish, and knowing who owns any company is rightly a matter of public concern.

12. How Important Are the Allocation Limits on New Share Issues?

The prospectus of British Telecom made it clear that it would be an offence for one individual to apply for more than a predetermined number of shares. This has now become standard practice for privatised companies.

The government's aim was to spread the ownership of shares as widely as possible and to be as fair as possible in a share issue expected to be oversubscribed. Where multiple applications were found, the standard practice was to allocate no shares to the person but to hold his cheques. The 'punishment' was effectively loss of interest on your money, and loss of opportunity to receive shares.

A harder line was taken with TSB employees who made multiple applications. By June 1987, 55 staff had been suspended.

A completely different approach was taken when it was subsequently discovered that Keith Best, then MP for Ynys Môn (Angelesey) and a barrister, had made multiple applications for British Telecom shares. In the first such case, he was prosecuted and sentenced to four months' imprisonment. To establish guidelines for the future, the appeal was heard by the Lord Chief Justice himself, who reduced it to a fine of £4,500, but made it clear that others found guilty could face imprisonment.

The tougher attitude was expressed by the original trial judge who said 'conduct of this kind is all too frequent and you and all those who may be considering behaving as you did must be made to realise that it does not pay'. At the appeal it was disclosed that 6,600 multiple applications for BT shares had been spotted, but only ten prosecutions brought. One person had made 1,000 applications.

Price Waterhouse, the accountants engaged to police the applications for BAA, used a new computer system called SMART (Suspect Multiple Applications Recording and Tracking). This first such use of computers enabled them to find a single network of 1,000 linked applications, and many smaller multiple applications. It certainly deterred others.

The firm also engaged the services of a handwriting expert, Derek Davies (who investigated evidence on Jack the Ripper). Every applicant who handed in a BAA application form at a receiving centre was recorded on video tape.

13. What is the Financial Services Act?

You'll be sorry you asked!

The Financial Services Act 1986 provides a regulatory framework for investment business. Some provisions became effective in 1986, but most provisions and most of the regulatory framework become fully effective in 1988.

The Act makes it a criminal offence to carry on an investment business (as defined) without a licence, and changes some investment regulations. As well as being a criminal offence, an unlicensed agreement will be unenforceable. This mirrors a provision of the Consumer Credit Act 1974 which proved effective in controlling hire purchase agreements.

The task of enforcing the new investment regulations is entrusted to the Securities and Investments Board (SIB) which was specially set up for this purpose.

A person conducting an investment business may be authorised in one of these ways:

1 directly from the SIB,
2 by membership of a self-regulating organisation (SRO),
3 certification by a recognised professional body (RPB).

The prospective SROs are:

1 Association of Futures Brokers and Dealers (AFBD),
2 Financial Intermediaries, Managers and Brokers Regulatory Association (FIMBRA),
3 Investment Management Regulatory Organisation (IMRO),
4 Life Assurance and Unit Trust Regulatory Organisation (LAUTRO),
5 Securities Association (a merger between the Stock Exchange and the International Securities Regulatory Organisation).

The RPBs are likely to include the Law Society (for solicitors) and the major accountancy bodies.

Corporate treasurers, public bodies and banks are generally exempt, but pension funds are not. There are special provisions for insurance companies, friendly societies, collective investment schemes and people authorised in another EEC country.

Under the Financial Services Act 1986, it will be an offence to make a misleading statement in connection with an advertisement; employees in an investment business must be 'fit and proper' people; and investors who lose money as a result of a breach of the SIB rules will be able to claim damages. The SIB also has powers to discipline investment businesses, to prevent employment of unsuitable people in those businesses, and to intervene in the conduct of business transacted by an authorised person. The SIB will also have powers to investigate companies.

15. What Happened on 19 October 1987?

1. What Happened

The markets 'crashed'.

On 16 October in New York the Dow-Jones index fell a record 108.36. On Monday 19 October, that record crash was surpassed by a spectacular fall of 508.32 points, more than double the Wall Street crash of 29 October 1929. The interdependence of world markets made it inevitable that such a crash would reverberate around the world, which it did to varying degrees. The FT-SE 100 index fell a record 250 points on 19 October.

2. The Background

The increase in share prices which began in 1975 accelerated during 1987. The year began with the FT-SE 100 index at 1679.0 and the Dow-Jones index at 1895.95. By the end of January 1987 the indices were 1832.8 and 2179.70, respectively. That is a 9 per cent increase in London and nearly a 15 per cent increase in New York. This increase continued throughout the first half of the year when new records were frequently being set, until by summer the FT-SE 100 index reached its all-time high of 2445 and the Dow-Jones 2722.42.

By early October 1987 the market appeared to have 'settled' and the FT-SE 100 index remained around 2350 and the Dow-Jones index around 2600. On 19 October 1987 the FT-SE 100 index fell from 2301.9 to 2052.3, and the Dow-Jones index fell from 2355.09 to 1738.40; falls of 10.8 per cent and 36.8 per cent respectively.

Increases and decreases generate their own momentum as dealers try to 'get ahead of the game'. Knowing that the market follows its own trends, dealers desperately tried to unload shares before the prices fell even further. This just further exacerbated the problem and pushed share prices even lower. On 26 October 1987 the Chancellor told the Stock Exchange 'the electronic automation and globalisation of the herd instinct is not an impressive sight'.

The fall continued in following weeks, despite a few false dawns when share prices briefly rallied. In the UK we talked of a 'crash'; in the US they talked of a 'meltdown'.

3. BP and the Hurricane

In the UK, the crash coincided with two other unprecedented events: a hurricane and the BP flotation.

In the early hours of 16 October the south of England was hit by a freak hurricane. Winds of up to 110 mph were the highest ever recorded and believed to be the worst at least since the great storm of 1703. The Stock Exchange was effectively closed for much of the day (for the first time in twenty years) as power supplies were disrupted and many staff were unable to get to work because roads and railways were blocked with fallen trees. Therefore, on Monday, the market effectively had two days' fall in one day.

The £7.2bn BP flotation was the world's biggest flotation ever. Indeed the government's £18.5m advertising campaign used the slogan 'and now for the big one'. The share price of 330p was announced on 15 October. Six million people had registered for priority forms. On the day of the announcement, BP's shares stood at 347p, so the offer price represented an attractive 5 per cent discount.

On 28 October when the offer closed, the share price was 259p. Surprisingly about 250,000 private investors still applied, but the underwriters were faced with losses of £1.5bn. The underwriters' request to postpone the issue (not surprisingly) met with little sympathy, but the government were nevertheless anxious not to add to the City's problems. A clever scheme was arranged whereby the Bank of England agreed, for a time, to buy the partly paid (120p) shares for at least 70p. This 'floor' provided a needed boost to City confidence, showing that the market and the economy can cope even with a unique combination of unprecedented adverse factors. (BP partly paid shares actually started trading at 85p.)

4. What Caused the Crash?

The villain of the piece was quickly named as the US government's budget deficit. What was not explained was why something which had existed for at least three years should suddenly cause such a crash.

It is easily overlooked that share prices are supposed to represent the value of a company. If a company has one billion shares priced at £2 each, the company is worth £2bn. You should be able to look at the company's accounts and see what supports that £2bn. The company might, for example, have net assets (buildings, plant, debtors, etc.) of £1.2bn, and profits of £100m a year which add perhaps another £800,000 goodwill to the value.

If those shares rise above £2, say to £2.50, and the extra 50p is not supported by assets, the company starts to become a 'bubble' which eventually bursts. Generally share prices trebled between 1982 and 1987. Allowing for inflation, this is a 140 per cent increase over five years: an increase of 19 per cent a year. The simple truth is that companies' values have just not increased by anything like that much: 3 per cent is nearer the truth.

A shake-out was inevitable – but it still caught people unawares.

5. How will it End?

If I knew that I would be furiously dealing in the market rather than writing this book! No one knows for certain, but we can learn something from history, particularly from the oil crash of 1986.

The price of oil, which stood at $33 a barrel in the early 1980s, halved in the first few months of 1986, falling to $9 a barrel by April 1986. The price recovered and remained around $18 in 1987. The price of oil simply returned to its inflation-adjusted price before the Arabs quadrupled it in the early 1970s. It returned to its 'real value'.

My view from Epsom in October 1987 is that the stock market will do the same. Having soared to unsupported heights, it will plunge to unrealistic lows, before settling at a 'real value' below that seen for most of 1987, but staying there for a while before gently increasing. But do remember that this is not an infallible prophecy!

6. So What Does the Private Investor Do?

Do not panic! If you bought before the crash, you have at worst lost the opportunity to make a quick profit. But that is not the main reason why you should have bought the shares in the first place. Your dividend income is unaffected by the excitement, as is your underlying security (the company's actual value). Even if you sold your British Telecom shares at the end of October 1987 at a low price, you would still show a greater return on your investment than if the money had been in a building society.

Also, while prices are low, investors can pick up real bargains.

Significantly, private investors generally have not panicked. The panic has been from option dealers, who in some cases have lost fortunes, and fund managers who compete with each other. The investor is not competing.

I believe that the October 1987 crash could in time prove to be very healthy for the country. Hopefully it will dampen down the less acceptable casino mentality of some punters, make investors take a longer term view of share ownership, and give the City the breathing space it needs to offer the private investor the service he deserves.

Appendix A
Stockbroking Firms

The following list is based solely on written replies to a
standard letter sent by the author. The omission of
information does not necessarily mean that a service is not
provided.

Commission rates quoted are for UK shares only. Generally
you can expect to pay less for dealings in gilts and unit trusts,
and more for dealings in foreign shares.

Adley Drew Ltd, 49 Doughty Street, London WC1N 2LF. *tel*:
01-831 9844.
> Licensed dealers in securities, specialising in unit trusts.
> Regular bulletins. Free advisory service. General
> commission rates not given but advice given for specific
> investments.

Ashton Tod McLaren, 13 Castle Street, Liverpool L2 4SU. *tel*:
051-236 8281.
> Full range of personal investment services. Commission
> at pre-Big Bang rates. Minimum commission £15.

Ashworth Sons and Barratt, Princes Chambers, 26 Pall Mall,
Manchester M2 1JS. *tel*: 061-832 4812.
> Private client firm, independent, specialise in
> Manchester-based firms. Detailed newsletters. Personal
> service. Commissions: to £7000: 1.65%; next £8000:
> 0.55%; to £125,000: 0.5%. Minimum commission £10.
> Other services.

Barratt and Cooke, 5/6 Opie Street, Norwich NR1 3DW. *tel*:
0603 624236.
> Only taking on new clients in Norfolk, Suffolk and
> Mansfield areas. Commission rate: to £7000: 1.5%;
> thereafter 0.5%. Minimum commission £12. No
> minimum portfolio. Free advice.

James Brearley and Sons, PO Box 34, 31 King Street, Blackpool FY1 3DQ. *tel*: 0253 21474.

Small firm which caters almost exclusively for private investors, particularly in Blackpool and Cumbria areas. Commission rates: first £7000: 1.5%; next £8000: 0.55%; thereafter 0.5% or negotiable. No minimum portfolio. Quarterly newsletter. Personal service. Clients are issued with an 'Investorcard' for straightforward dealing.

Brewin Dolphin & Co., 5 Giltspur Street, London EC1A 9DE. *tel*: 01-248 4400.

Personal and comprehensive service offered to small client. Newsletters. No minimum portfolio size as such, but size and commission negotiated with client.

Broadbridge Lawson & Co., 16 Park Place, Leeds LS1 2SJ. *tel*: 0532 443721.

Caters almost exclusively for private investors. Commission rates appear to be the same as for pre-Big Bang. Minimum commission £9 for deals up to £200, otherwise £12. Discretionary portfolios and other services provided. Useful literature provided free to clients. Newsletters.

Brown Shipley Asset Management Ltd, 2/3 Eldon Street, London EC2M 7DU. *tel*: 01-337 1099.

Merchant bank that provides for private investors through subsidiaries. Generally minimum managed portfolio £100,000; unit trust portfolio £10,000. Personal service. Free advice. Newsletters. Managed portfolios subject to charges on top of commission rates (which were not advised).

Buckmaster and Moore, 80 Cannon Street, London EC4N 6HH. *tel*: 01-588 2868.

Comprehensive and personal services. Commission at pre-Big Bang rates. Helpful literature provided. Friendly personal service. Good research facilities.

Butler and Briscoe, 3 College Green, Dublin 2. *tel*: Dublin 777348.

Minimum portfolio size £25,000. Commission at 1.65%.

Cazenove, 12 Tokenhouse Yard, London EC2R 7AN. *tel*: 01-588 2828.

Only interested in client portfolios of 'a substantial size'.

Charterhouse Investment Management Ltd, 6 New Bridge Street, London EC4V 6JH. *tel*: 01-248 4000.

Portfolio management service between £50,000 and £100,000; full management service above £100,000. Below £50,000 unit trust services available. Management fees charged on portfolio size 0.88% to £500,000, thereafter 0.5%. Minimum fee £450. Comprehensive services. Investment newsletter.

R.A. Coleman & Co., 204 High Street, Bangor, Gwynedd LL57 1NY. *tel*: 0248 353242

Entirely private clients. Commission: first £5000: 1.65%; next £2000: 1.5%; next £13,000: 0.5%. Minimum commission £12.50. Two newsletters a year. Free advice. Personal service.

Henry Cooke Lumsden, Byrom House, Quay Street, Manchester M3 3JD. *tel*: 061-834 2332.

Two-thirds of business is from private clients. Commission rates are pre-Big Bang. Minimum portfolio usually £5000. Two-monthly client bulletins. Personal service. Also offered a cheaper market-dealing only service called 'MarketLink'. MarketLink commissions: first £7000: 1.5%; next £8000: 0.4%. Minimum commission up to £50: £5; £50-£100: £8; thereafter £10. This service is not being offered to new investors.

T.C. Coombs & Co., 4-5 Bonhill Street, London EC2A 4BX. *tel*: 01-588 6209.

Commission rates not given. Detailed newsletter.

Coutts & Co, 440 Strand, London WC2R 0QS. *tel*: 01-379 6262.

Asset management service for customers with at least £250,000 of easily realisable assets.

DF Financial Services, 1 Serjeants' Inn, London EC4Y 1JD. *tel*: 01-353 2000.

Minimum portfolio £25,000. Fees charged for work at £10 to £60 an hour but may be mitigated by commission earned. Initial interview free. Personal service. Newsletters.

Dennis Murphy Campbell & Co., 2 Russia Row, London EC2V 8BP. *tel*: 01-726 8631.

Specialise in private investment. Commissions as pre-Big

Bang. Minimum commission £10. No minimum portfolio, but will not take occasional orders below £500. Occasional newsletters. Personal service. Advice, valuations, etc. are free.

Earnshaw Haes and Sons, 17 Tokenhouse Yard, London EC2R 7LB. *tel*: 01-588 5699.
Commissions at pre-Big Bang rates. No minimum portfolio, but £25,000 minimum for discretionary management. Newsletters. Personal service.

Fidelity Investment Services Ltd, River Walk, Tonbridge, Kent TN9 1DY. Call-free telephones: 0800 414161 for enquiries and investment advice; 0800 414181 for dealing.
Seven-day dealing service. Commission rates not given. Many facilities offered to private investor. Portfolio monitor service £7500 minimum (in unit trusts). Managed portfolio service minimum £10,000.

Fielding Newson-Smith & Co., Garrard House, 31 Gresham Street, London EC2V 7DX. *tel*: 01-606 7711.
Discretionary portfolio minimum £50,000.

Foster and Braithwaite, 22 Austin Friars, London EC2N 2BU. *tel*: 01-588 6111.
Only deals with private investors. Detailed newsletter. Pre-Big Bang commission rates; minimum commission £10.

Fowler Sutton & Co. Ltd, PO Box 10, 35 Bishop Lane, Hull HU1 1NZ. *tel*: 0482 27570.
Offers standard service, discretionary portfolio service and a dealing only service (at reduced commissions). Quarterly newsletter. Personal service and other facilities.

Fyshe Horton Finney & Co. Charles House, 148–149 Great Charles Street, Birmingham B3 3HT. *tel*: 021-236 3111.
Personal service. Commission 1.5% to £7000; 0.5% on next £8000; 0.25% to £250,000; thereafter negotiable. Minimum charge on purchases £15; minimum charge on sales – under £200: £6, £200 +: £10; discretionary management: flat charge £15 plus 0.5% annual charge for portfolio below £250,000, 0.25% above. Newsletter. Comprehensive services.

Gilbert Jeffs and Co. Ltd, 14 Bennetts Hill, Birmingham B2 5SE. *tel*: 021-643 7861.

Caters mainly for private investors. Commission rates: first £4000: 1.75%; next £4000: 1%; next £7000: 0.5%; thereafter 0.25%. Minimum commission £15. Reduced rates for deals under £100. Commissions may be higher if split with an intermediary. Newsletters. Personal service. Free advice.

Goodbody James Capel, 5 College Green, Dublin 2. *tel*: Dublin 793888.

Largest private investor base of any firm. Now 40% owned by James Capel. Personal service. Detailed newsletters, booklets and share information. Commission 1.65%; minimum commission £20. Discretionary services for portfolios from £20,000.

Greenwell Montagu, Bow Bells House, Bread Street, London EC4M 9EL. *tel*: 01-248 0702.

Personal service. Commission at pre-Big Bang rates. No minimum portfolio, though £50,000 diversified recommended. Newsletter.

Greig Middleton, 78 Old Broad Street, London EC2M 1JE. *tel*: 01-920 0481.

Caters for private individuals. Commission rates: 1.65% on first £7000; 0.5% on next £11,000, 0.4% to £75,000; 0.3% to £200,000; 0.25% to £500,000. Minimum commissions from £2 to £15. Minimum portfolio £10,000. Friendly personal service. Newsletters.

Hanson and Co., Auckland House, 109 Thorne Road, Doncaster DN2 5BA. *tel*: 0302 340200.

Comprehensive range of services.

Hill Osborne, Royal Insurance Building, Silver Street, Lincoln LN2 1DU. *tel*: 0522 28244.

Personal service. Commission: 1.65% to £7000; 0.55% on next £8000; 0.5% on balance. Minimum commission £12.50. Newsletter. Comprehensive services.

Hoare Govett, Heron House 319/325 High Holborn, London WC1V 7PB. *tel*: 01-404 0344.

>Comprehensive services. Operates a 'dealercall' card service at these reduced commission rates: to £7000: 1.25%; to £25000: 0.45%; to £250,000: 0.35%; above 0.25%. Minimum commission £12.50.

Hoare Govett (Channel Islands) Ltd, PO Box 1, 35 Don Street, St Helier, Jersey. *tel*: 0534 73311.

>Particularly geared up to serve expatriate and non-resident clients. Personal service. Discretionary portfolio management from £50,000. Offshore funds account from £10,000, or savings plan from £250 a month.

James Capel, PO Box 551, 6 Bevis Marks, London EC3A 7JQ. *tel*: 01-621 0011.

>Largest firm of stockbrokers. Commission: 1.65% to £7000; 0.55% on next £8000; 0.5% thereafter; minimum commission £20. Minimum portfolio £500 (unit trusts). Minimum discretionary managed portfolio £75,000. Comprehensive other services.

Keith Bayley Rogers and Co., 194–200 Bishopsgate, London EC2M 4NR. *tel*: 01-623 2400.

>Quarterly newsletter. Personal service. Comprehensive services. Independent (and proud of it). Commission rates not given.

Kleinwort Grieveson, 10 Fenchurch Street, London EC3 3LB. *tel*: 01-623 8000.

>Commission at pre-Big Bang rates. Minimum commission £35 (purchases), £30 (sales). Discretionary management on portfolios from £100,000. Up to March 1987 the firm also operated a 'ShareCall' card service for straightforward dealing at a commission rate of 1% subject to a minimum of £12 and a maximum of £100. This has now been suspended. Other services offered.

Laing and Cruikshank, 7 Copthall Avenue, London EC2R 7BE. *tel*: 01-588 2800.

>Claim to be largest private client stockbroker, but refused to give details of commission charges or services.

Laws and Co. Ltd, 40 Queen Square, Bristol BS1 4DU. *tel*: 0272 293901.

Part of Allied Provincial Securities Ltd. Personal service. Commission: 1.65% on first £4000; 1.5% on next £3000; 0.5% on next £8000; £0.35% on next £35,000; 0.25% above £50,000. Minimum commission £10 to £15 depending on size. No minimum portfolio but management below £10,000 is discouraged. Other services.

Le Masurier James and Chinn Ltd, 29 Broad Street, St Helier, Jersey. *tel*: 0534 72825.

Oldest stockbroking business in the Channel Islands. Commission at pre-Big Bang rates. Minimum commissions £5 to £15.

Lyddon, 2–6 Austin Friars, London EC2N 2EE. *tel*: 01-628 5573. Also 113 Bute Street, Cardiff CF1 1QS. *tel*: 0222 480000. Also 33 Mansel Street, Swansea SA1 1EB. *tel*: 0792 475111.

Personal service. Commission: up to £400: (buying) £12, (selling) £3 to £12; to £848: £14; to £7000: 1.65%; next £8000: 0.55%, next £115,000: 0.5%. A main activity is portfolio management, minimum £15,000. Newsletter.

L. Messel & Co., 9A Devonshire Square, London EC2M 4YL. *tel*: 01-626 9561.

Portfolios from £40,000. Commission: rates not given. Portfolios also subject to 'department charges': from £40,000 to £100,000: 0.25%; to £200,000: £250; to £500,000: 0.125%.

Milton Mortimer & Co., 109A High Street, Barnstaple. *tel*: 0271 71199.

Concentrates on private clients. Commissions at pre-Big Bang rates. Minimum commission £12, but discretionary for deals less than £100. No minimum portfolio size though £10,000 recommended. For discretionary management £25,000 minimum recommended. Free advice. Quarterly newsletter. Personal service.

Murray & Co. Stockbrokers Ltd, 94/96 Newhall Street, Birmingham B3 1PE. *tel*: 021-236 0552.

Part of Allied Provincial Services. Commission at pre-Big Bang rates. Minimum portfolio of £25,000. Minimum commission £10. Comprehensive range of other services. Personal service. Investment newsletters. Good research facilities.

Neilson Milnes, Martins Building, 4 Water Street, Liverpool L2 3UF. *tel*: 051-236 6666.
Caters specifically for private investors. Commission 1.65%. Minimum commission £15. No minimum portfolio size though investors are encouraged to deal in amounts of £500 plus. Newsletter. Personal service. Other facilities.

Penney Easton & Co., 24 George Square, Glasgow, G2 1EB. *tel*: 041-248 2911.
Specialises in services to the private client. Commission at pre-Big Bang rates. Minimum commission £12. No minimum portfolio though £15,000 recommended. Discretionary management service subject to additional charges. Free advice. Personal service. Newsletter.

Phillips and Drew, Mercury House, Triton Court, Finsbury Square, London EC2A 1PD. *tel*: 01-628 4444.
Commissions at pre-Big Bang rates. Minimum commission £20 (purchases), £10 (sales). Offers 'Share Service' at same commission rates. Comprehensive range of other services.

Quilter Goodison Company, 31–45 Gresham Street, London EC2V 7LH. *tel*: 01-600 4177.
Commission rates: first £10,000: 1.2%. Minimum commission £12.50. For 'dealing desk' services (which includes advice, and other securities), commission is 1.4% subject to a minimum of £15. Managed service for portfolios from £2500. Discretionary service for portfolios from £25,000. Other facilities.

Ramsey Crookall and Co., 25 Athol Street, Douglas, Isle of Man. *tel*: 0624 73171.
Commission: first £8000: 1.5%; next £92,000: 0.5%; next £200,000: 0.4%; next £200,000: 0.3%; next 0.25%; above £1m: 0.125%. Minimum commission: £10 to £15 depending on size.

Redmayne Bentley, Merton House, 84 Albion Street, Leeds LS1 6AG. *tel*: 0532 436941.

Most business is private client based. Commission rates: first £7000 1.5%; next £13000 0.5%; thereafter negotiable. Minimum commission £10 (£8 if transaction below £250). No minimum portfolio but £5000 for managed portfolios.

Rensburg, Silkhouse Court, Tithebarn Street, Liverpool L2 2NH. *tel*: 051-227 2030.

About 90 per cent of business is for private investors. Free advice. Newsletters. Personal service. No minimum portfolio though £5000 recommended. Commission at pre-Big Bang rates.

Richardson Chubb Love Rogers, 37 Castle Street, Salisbury, Wilts SP1 1UB. *tel*: 0722 335211.

Personal service. Newsletters. Commission: 1.65% up to £7000; 0.55% on next £8000; 0.5% on next £115,000. Minimum commission £15. Minimum discretionary unit management £10,000. Other services.

Sabin Bacon White & Co., 33 Great Charles Street, Queensway, Birmingham B3 3JW. *tel*: 021-200 1122.

Up to 90 per cent of business is for private clients. Commission rates: first £3500: 1.65%; next £3500: 1.25%; next £5000: 0.5%; above £12000: 0.25%. Minimum commission £15 (purchases), £10 (sale). Personal service. Newsletter.

Schaverien & Co., 18½ Sekforde Street, London EC1R OHN. *tel*: 01-251 1626.

Commission rates – for execution service only: first £10,000: 1.25%; above £10,000: 0.5%. For standard portfolio service: first £7000: 1.65%; thereafter 0.55%. Discretionary service starts at 2%. Minimum commission (all services) £15, except £10 for deals up to £100. Newsletter. Personal service.

Albert E. Sharp & Co., Edmund House, 12 Newhall Street, Birmingham B3 3ER. *tel*: 021-236 5801.

Very interested in private investors. Personal service. Commission: first £1500: 2.0%; next £6500: 1.25%; above £8000: 0.25%. Minimum commission: £15 (purchase), £10 (sale), £5 (sale under £100).

Shaw & Co., 4 London Wall Buildings, Blomfield Street, London EC2M 5NT. *tel*: 01-638 6344.

Specialise in private client services.Commissions at pre-Big Bang rates. Minimum commission £15. Extra £5 per transaction charged if nominee service used. No minimum portfolio but regard £20,000 as 'appropriate' for the advisory service. Newsletter. Personal service.

Sheppards, 1 London Bridge, London SE1 9QU. *tel*: 01-378 7000.

Advisory services offered. Commission rates not given. Detailed newsletter. Free advice.

Spencer Thornton, 29 Throgmorton Street, London EC2N 2JU. *tel*: 01-236 9353.

Private business is about 80 per cent of work. Personal service. Commission rates as pre-Big Bang. Minimum portfolio £20,000, for discretionary management: £50,000. Also offered is a 'no frills dealing service' with 'Spencercall' service, whose commission rate is 1% subject to a minimum of £12. Can offer detailed research and advice on international markets.

Stancliffe Ltd, D Floor, Milburn House, Newcastle upon Tyne, NE1 1LZ. *tel*: 091-232 6695.

Services geared to private investor. Member of Allied Provincial Services. Commission rates: transactions to £199: £10 (purchases), £2 to £10 (sales); from £200 to £909: £12 to £15. No minimum portfolio for either discretionary or non-discretionary handling. Free advice. Personal service.

Stock Beech, Bristol and West Building, Broad Quay, Bristol BS1 4DD. *tel*: 0272 20051.

Commission rates: first £7500: 1.65%; to £50,000: 0.5%; to £100,000: 0.25%. Higher fees (starting at 1.8%) for discretionary management. Minimum commission £15. No minimum portfolio though transactions below £500 are not recommended. Advisory service for portfolios from £10,000; discretionary management from £20,000. Newsletter. Personal service.

R.L. Stott and Co. (IOM) Ltd, 54–58 Athol Street, Douglas, Isle of Man. *tel*: 0624 73701.

Offshore firm catering for private investor. Commission rates not given. Minimum portfolio normally £25,000. Free advice. Personal service. First newsletter due late 1987.

Strauss Turnbull & Co. Ltd, Moorgate Place, London EC2R 6HR. *tel*: 01-638 5699.

Commission: to £7000: 1.65%; to £125,000: 0.5%. Minimum commission: (up to £200) £6; (£200 and above) £12. Newsletters. Other services.

Vivian Gray, Ling House, 10–13 Dominion Street, London EC2M 2UX. *tel*: 01-638 0075.

Mainly concerned with providing a personal service to private investors. Commissions at pre-Big Bang rates, but rates can be negotiated for a dealing only service. No minimum portfolio. Free investment service. Monthly newsletter. Personal service.

Walker Crips Weddle Beck & Co., Kemp House, 152/160 City Road, London EC1V 2PQ. *tel*: 01-253 7502.

About half of its business is for private investors. Commission rates: to £5000: 1.65%; to £7000: 1.25%; above £7000: 0.5%. Minimum commission £15 (but lower rates for deals below £500). Minimum portfolio £20,000. Direct dealing service offered through 'Investorlink' at a commission rate of 1%. Applicants must apply in writing. Quarterly newsletter. Personal service.

Westlake and Co, Princess House, Eastlake Walk, Plymouth PL1 1HG. *tel*: 0752 220971.

Commission rates: first £4000: 1.65%; next £3000: 1.5%; next £8000: 0.5%; next £35,000: 0.35%; thereafter 0.25%. Minimum portfolio £30,000; minimum discretionary portfolio £50,000.

Whale Hardaway & Co. Ltd, 5 Park Hill Road, Torquay, Devon TQ1 2AN. *tel*: 0803 22441.

Ninety per cent of all business is private. Commission at pre-Big Bang rates. Minimum commission £12. No minimum portfolio size. Free advice. Personal service. Newsletter.

Wilshere Baldwin & Co., 19 The Crescent, King Street,
Leicester. LE1 6RX. *tel*: 0533 541344.
>Commission at pre-Big Bang rates. No minimum
>portfolio. Personal service. Newsletter.

Wise Speke, Commercial Union House, 39 Pilgrim Street,
Newcastle upon Tyne NE1 6RQ. *tel*: 091-261 1266.
>Primarily a private client firm. Commission rates: first
>£7000: 1.65%; next £8000: 0.55%; next £115,000: 0.5%;
>next £170,000: 0.4%. Minimum commission £12 (though
>rates down to £2.50 apply to deals below £250).
>Newsletter. Personal service.

Appendix B: Personal Equity Plan Schemes

Allied Provincial Ltd
    PO Box 84, City House, 206/208 Marton Road,
    Middlesborough, Cleveland TS4 2JE. *tel*: 0642 225423.

S.P. Angel & Co.
    Moorgate Hall, 155–157 Moorgate, London EC2M 6XB.
    tel: 01-588 3427.

Arnold Stansby & Co.
    Dennis House, Marsden Street, Manchester M2 3JJ.
    tel: 061-832 8554.

Ashton Tod McLaren
    13 Castle Street, Liverpool. *tel*: 051-236 8281.

A.T. Savings Ltd
    Meadow House, 64 Reform Street, Dundee DD1 1TJ.
    tel: 0382 21234.

Bank of Scotland
    The Mold, Edinburgh, EH1 1YZ. *tel*: 031-442 7777.

Bannerbush Ltd
    134a Uxbridge Road, London W12 8AA. *tel*: 01-749 6282.

Barclayshare Ltd
    Iveco-Ford House, Watford WD1 1SR. *tel*: 0923-46333.

Baring Investment Management Ltd
    8 Bishopsgate, London EC2N 4AE. *tel*: 01-283 8833.

Battye Wimpenny and Dawson
    Woodsome House, Woodsome Park, Fenay Bridge,
    Huddersfield HD8 0JG. *tel*: 0484 608066.

Bell Houldsworth Ltd
> GPO Box 329, Stock Exchange Buildings, 4 Norfolk Street, Manchester M60 2QL. *tel*: 061-834 3542.

Bell Lawrie Ltd
> PO Box 8, Erskine House, 68 Queen Street, Edinburgh EH2 4AE. *tel*: 031-225 2566.

Blankstone Sington & Co.
> Martins Buildings, 6 Water Street, Liverpool L2 3SP. *tel*: 051-227 1881.

Brewin Dolphin & Co.
> 5 Giltspur Street, London EC1A 9DE. *tel*: 01-248 4400.

Broker Financial Services Investment Management Ltd
> 127 High Street, Oxford OX1 4DF. *tel*: 04862 29099.

W. & J. Burness WS
> 16 Hope Street, Charlotte Square, Edinburgh EH2 4DD. *tel*: 031-226 2561.

CGA (Trustee & Investment) Co. Ltd
> Icknield Way West, Letchworth, Hertfordshire SG6 4AP. *tel*: Letchworth 682377.

Capel-Cure Myers
> 65 Holborn Viaduct, London EC1A 2EA. *tel*: 01-236 5080.

Castle Cairn (Financial Services) Ltd
> 64 Queen Street, Edinburgh EH2 4NA. *tel*: 031-225 2092.

Cawood Smithis & Co.
> 22 East Parade, Harrogate, North Yorkshire, HG1 5LT. *tel*: 0423 66781.

Charterhall Management Services Ltd
> 4 Highfield Road, Edgbaston, Birmingham B15 3EH. *tel*: 021-455 7133.

C. Hoare & Co.
> 37 Fleet Street, London EC4P 4DQ. *tel*: 01-353 4522.

Christian von Conzendorff-Mattner
> Parkhill House, 1 Parkhill Road, Torquay TQ1 2AL. *tel*: Torquay 214313.

Coutts and Co.
15 Lombard Street, London EC3V 9AV. *tel*: 01-379 6262.

Josias Cunningham & Co.
2 Bridge Street, Belfast, BT1 1NX. *tel*: 0232 246005.

Dartington and Co. Ltd
Central Offices, Skinners Bridge, Dartington, Totnes, Devon TQ9 6JE. *tel*: 0803 862271.

Dexter & Co. Financial Services Ltd
Rollestone House, Bridge Street, Horncastle, Lincolnshire LN9 5HZ. *tel*: Horncastle 6071.

Douglas J. Townley & Co.
70a Lee Lane, Harwich, Bolton, Greater Manchester BL6 7AE.

Duncan Lawrie Ltd
1 Hobart Place, London SW1W 0HU. *tel*: 01-245 9321.

Eagle Star Trust Co. Ltd
1 Threadneedle Street, London EC2R 8BE. *tel*: 01-493 8411.

Edinburgh Fund Management plc
4 Melville Crescent, Edinburgh EH3 7JB. *tel*: 031-226 4931.

F.S. Investment Managers
190 West George Street, Glasgow G2 2PA. *tel*: 041-332 3132.

Fidelity Nominees Ltd
River Walk, Tonbridge, Kent TN9 2RH. *tel*: 0732 361144.

James Finlay Corporation Ltd
Finlay House, 10–14 West Nile Street, Glasgow G1 2PP. *tel*: 041-204 1321.

J.L. Fisher & Co.
45 Chiswick Common Road, London W4 1RZ.

Framlington Investment Management Ltd
3 London Wall Buildings, London EC2M 5NQ. *tel*: 01-628 5181.

Fraser Henderson Ltd
20 Chiswell Street, London EC1Y 4TY. *tel*: 01-628 0241.

Gartmore Investment Management Ltd
2 St Mary Avenue, London EC3A 8BP. *tel*: 01-623 1212.

Peter H. Gartside
c/o Gartside and Trippier Ltd, 2 Old Bank Chambers, St
Ann's Square, Manchester M2 7PF. *tel*: 061-834 6084.

Ginn Reijs Investment Management Ltd
Castle House, London Road, Tunbridge Wells, Kent TN1
1BX. *tel*: 0892 34433.

Granville & Co. Ltd
8 Lovat Lane, London EC3R 8BP. *tel*: 01-621 1212.

Grenfell and Colegrave Ltd
55/61 Moorgate, London EC2R 6DR. *tel*: 01-628 6044.

Hastings Consultants Ltd
25 East Street, Farnham, Surrey GU9 7SD. *tel*: 0252
710565.

Harvard Securities plc
Harvard House, 42–44 Dolben Street, London SE1 0UQ.
tel: 01-928 8691.

Henderson Administration Ltd
26 Finsbury Square, London EC2A 1DA. *tel*: 01-638 5757.

Heseltine Moss & Co.
30–31 Friar Street, Reading RG1 1AH. *tel*: 0734 595511.

Hichens Harrison & Co.
Bell Court House, 11 Blomfield Street, London EC2M
1LB. *tel*: 01-588 5171.

Hill Osborne & Co.
Royal Insurance Building, Silver Street, Lincoln LN2
1DU. *tel*: 0522 28244.

Hill Samuel & Co. Ltd
100 Wood Street, London. *tel*: 01-686 4355.

Hoare Govett Financial Services Ltd
Heron House, 319/325 High Holborn, London WC1V
7PB. *tel*: 01-404 0344.

I.A. Pritchard
National Westminster Bank Building, 1 Richmond Hill,
The Square, Bournemouth BH2 6HW. *tel*: 0202 297035.

Individual Pension Funds Ltd
    4 Memorial Road, Walkden, Manchester M28 5AQ.
    tel: 061-790 1816.

Roy James & Co.
    Stock Exchange Buildings, 33 Great Charles Street,
    Queensway, Birmingham B3 3JS. *tel*: 021-236 8131.

James Capel & Co.
    James Capel House, PO Box 551, 6 Bevis Marks, London
    EC3A 7JQ. *tel*: 01-621 0496.

Jarvis Investment Management Ltd
    1 The Drive, Warwick Park, Tunbridge Wells, Kent TN2
    5ER. *tel*: 0892 36538.

J. Edward Sellars and Partners Ltd
    17 Portland Square, Bristol BS2 8SJ. *tel*: 0272 429491.

John Siddall & Son
    The Stock Exchange, 4 Norfolk Street, Manchester M2
    1DS. *tel*: 061-832 7471.

Leopold Joseph and Sons Ltd
    31–45 Greshman Street, London EC2V 7EA. *tel*: 01-588
    2323.

Laing and Cruikshank
    Piercy House, 7 Copthall Avenue, London EC2R 7BE.
    tel: 01-588 2800.

Julian Lang Financial Services Ltd
    St Helen's, 1 Undershaft, London EC3A 8JR. *tel*: 01-623
    1026.

Kleinwort Grieveson Investment Management Ltd
    20 Fenchurch Street, London EC3P 3DB. *tel*: 01-623 8000.

Lamont and Partners Ltd
    48 Charles Street, Berkeley Square, London W1X 7PB.
    tel: 01-629 4509.

Laurence Keen & Co.
    Basildon House, 7–11 Moorgate, London EC2R 6AH.
    tel: 01-600 9100.

Legal and General (Investment Management) Ltd
Temple Court, 11 Queen Victoria Street, London EC4N
4TP. *tel*: 01-248 9678.

Lindsays WS
11 Atholl Crescent, Edinburgh, EH3 8HE.

Linenhall Financial Services
1–3 Lombard Street, Belfast BT1 1RB. *tel*: 0232 249156.

Lloyds Bank plc
Personal Equity Plan Centre, Capital House, 1/5
Perrymount Road, Haywards Heath, West Sussex RH16
3SP. *tel*: 01-623 1288.

Lonsdale Chetwyn Holdings Ltd
10a North Street, Carshalton, Surrey SM5 2HU.

MIM Ltd
11 Devonshire Square, London EC2M 4YR. *tel*: 01-588
2777.

R.N. McKean & Co.
11 Grove Place, Bedford MK40 3JJ. *tel*: Bedford 51131.

Marksmen Financial Management Ltd
14/15 Fitzhardinge Street, London W1H 9PL.

Midland Bank Trust Co. Ltd
Head Office, 6 Threadneedle Street, London EC2R 8BB.
tel: 01-260 8000.

Phillip J. Milton & Co.
4 Taw Vale, Barnstaple, North Devon. *tel*: 0271 44300.

Miton Investments Ltd
7 Portland Place, London W1N 3AA. *tel*: 01-631 0906.

Murray Beith and Murray WS
39 Castle Street, Edinburgh EH2 3BH.

Murray Cowles Associates Ltd
92 Fleet Street, London EC4Y 1DH *tel*: 01-583 1633.

National Westminster Bank plc
c/o Travers Smith and Braithwaite, 6 Snow Hill, London.
tel: 01-726 1000.

New Life Financial Services Ltd
    31 Oxford Street, Southampton, Hants SO1 1DN.
    tel: 0703 334727.

Newby Investment Consultants Ltd
    Midland Bank Chambers, New Market Street, Ulverston
    LA12 7LH.

Pagan Osborne and Grace
    12 St Catherine Street, Cupar, Fife KY15 4HN.

Perpetual Portfolio Management Ltd
    48 Hart Street, Henley-on-Thames, Oxon RG9 2AZ.
    tel: 0491 576868.

Phillips and Drew Investment Services Ltd
    Mercury House, Triton Court, 14 Finsbury Square,
    London EC2A 1PD. *tel*: 01-628 4444.

Pilling Trippier & Co.
    12 St Ann's Square, Manchester M2 7HT. *tel*: 061-832
    6581.

Pointon York Ltd
    7 Cavendish Square, London W1M 9HA. *tel*: 01-631 3015.

P.H. Pope and Son
    6 Pall Mall, Hanley, Stroke-on-Trent. *tel*: 0782 25154.

Professional Link Services Ltd
    Hinton Buildings, Hinton Road, Bournemouth BH1 2EF.
    tel: 0202 292161.

Prudential Portfolio Managers Ltd
    142 Holborn Bars, London EC1N 2NH. *tel*: 01-478 3377.

Puma Securities Ltd
    Messrs Kramers, Park House, 26 North End Road,
    London NW11 7PT. *tel*: 01-408 0250.

Quilter Goodison Co.
    PO Box 216, Garrard House, 31–45 Gresham Street,
    London EC2V 7LH. *tel*: 01-600 4177.

Robert Ramsden & Co.
    PO Box B16, 1st Floor, Estate Buildings, Railway Street,
    Huddersfield, HD1 1NE. *tel*: 0484 21501.

Raphael Zorn
10 Throgmorton Avenue, London EC2N 2DP. *tel*: 01-628 4000.

Rathbone Bros & Co.
Port of Liverpool Building, Pier Head, Liverpool L3 1NW. *tel*: 051-236 8674.

Redmayne Bentley
Merton House, 84 Albion Street, Leeds LS1 6AG. *tel*: 0532 436941.

Reigate Asset Management Ltd
Lonsdale House, 7–11 High Street, Reigate, Surrey RH2 9AA. *tel*: 07372 44869.

Rensburg
9th floor, Silkhouse Court, Tithebarn Street, Liverpool L2 2NH. *tel*: 051-227 2030.

Ringley Financial Counselling
Ringley House, London Road, Reigate, Surrey RH2 9QH. *tel*: Reigate 45485.

Save and Prosper Group Ltd
Administration Centre, Hexagon House, 28 Western Road, Romford, Essex RM1 3LB. *tel*: Romford 6696.

Schroder Securities Ltd
120 Cheapside, London EC2V 6DS. *tel*: 0705 827733.

Sentinel Portfolio Management
30 City Road, London EC1Y 7AY.

Shaw & Co.
4 London Wall Buildings, Blomfield Street, London EC2M 5NT. *tel*: 01-638 3644.

Albert E. Sharp & Co.
Edmund House, 12 Newhall Street, Birmingham B3 3ER. *tel*: 021-236 5801.

Sheppards
No. 1 London Bridge, London SE1 9QU. *tel*: 01-378 7000.

Silkbarn Management Ltd
Lancaster House, Mercury Court, Tithebarn Street, Liverpool L2 2QP. *tel*: 051-227 2782.

Singer and Friedlander Ltd
    21 New Street, Bishopsgate, London EC2M 4HR.
    tel: 01-623 3000.

Smith and Williamson Securities
    1 Riding House Street, London W1A 3AS. *tel*: 01-637
    5377.

Spencer Thornton & Co.
    Warnford Court, 29 Throgmorton Street, London EC2N
    4HQ. *tel*: 01-628 4411.

Stanecastle Assets Ltd
    43 Charlotte Square, Edinburgh EH2 4HQ. *tel*: 031-225
    7685.

Star Financial Services Ltd
    40 Gloucester Road, North Harrow, Middlesex HA1
    4PW.

Stirling and Gilmour
    24 Gilmour Street, Alexandria, Dunbartonshire G83 0DB.

Stock Beech and Co. Ltd
    The Bristol and West Building, Broad Quay, Bristol BS1
    4DD. *tel*: Bristol 20051.

Sutton Fowler & Co. Ltd
    PO Box 10, 35 Bishop Lane, Hull HU1 1NZ. *tel*: Hull
    25750.

TSB Scotland, Financial Advisory Services Department
    PO Box 713, Orchard Brae House, 30 Queensferry Road,
    Edinburgh EH4 2UL. *tel*: 0264 56789.

T.S. Portfolio Ltd
    3 Lonsdale Gardens, Tunbridge Wells, Kent TN1 1NX.
    tel: 0892 510000.

Topino Ltd
    21 Queensdale Place, Holland Park, London W11 4SQ.

Touche Remnant Financial Management Ltd
    Mermaid House, 2 Puddle Dock, London EC4V 3AT.
    tel: 01-236 8181.

Tower Fund Managers Ltd
    Tower House, 5–11 Mortimer Street, London W1N 7RH.
    tel: 01-580 0617.

Vivian Gray & Co.
Ling House, 10–13 Dominion Street, London EC2M 2UX. *tel*: 01-638 2888.

Walker Crips Weddle Beck & Co.
Kemp House, 152/160 City Road, London EC1V 2PQ. *tel*: 01-253 7502.

Williams de Broe Hill Chaplin & Co. Ltd
PO Box 515, Pinners Hall, Austin Friars, London EC2P 2HS. *tel*: 01-588 7511.

Windsor Investment Management Ltd
Windsor House, 83 Kingsway, London WC2B 6SD. *tel*: 01-831 7373.

Wise Speke & Co.
Commercial Union House, 39 Pilgrim Street, Newcastle upon Tyne NE1 6RQ. *tel*: 091-261 1266.

Yorkshire Bank
20 Merrion Way, Leeds LS2 8NZ. *tel*: 0532 441244.

Note: This appendix lists plan managers approved by the Inland Revenue as at 12 December 1986. Since it was compiled other schemes have been authorised including Abbey National, who have joined up with Fidelity and Bradford and Bingley, who have joined up with James Capel.

Glossary

'A' shares
> Ordinary shares but with different voting rights, usually none. Occasionally companies also have 'B', 'C' shares, etc.

AB
> Abbreviation of *'Aktiebolag'*, Swedish for 'limited company'

AG
> Abbreviation of *'Aktiengesellschaft'*, German or Austrian equivalent of a public limited company.

A/S
> Abbreviation of either *'Aktieselskab'*, Danish public company, or *'Aksjeselskap'*, Norwegian public company.

AGM
> Abbreviation for **annual general meeting**.

account
> **1** The Stock Exchange period (usually two weeks) in which shares are traded.
> **2** Record of financial transactions disclosing amounts owed and payments received.

accumulation units
> Additional units applied to a unit trust (or similar) in lieu of interest.

actuals
> A physical **commodity** as opposed to futures.

ad valorem duty
> Stamp duty payable at an amount relative to the size of the underlying transaction, as opposed to **fixed duty**.

allotment
> The process by which the investor becomes the legal owner of the shares.

allotment letter
> A letter to a potential investor advising him what shares have been allotted to him, subject to payment.

alpha coefficient
> The measure by which all shares are shown to be subject to general economic trends. A movement which is peculiar to specific shares or classes of shares is the **beta factor**.

alpha shares
> The most widely traded shares.

amber light
> Advance warning of problems in a company.

ambulance stocks
> Recommended investments for reviving a poorly performing portfolio.

annual general meeting
> The meeting which every company must have by law. All shareholders are invited to attend, to vote on various matters and may ask questions.

application
> The process by which an investor subscribes for shares.

appropriation
> Where more units in a unit trust are being bought than sold.

arb
> Colloquial name for an *arbitrageur*.

arbitrage
> Trading in the same item (e.g. stocks, currency) but in different markets with a view to making a profit on price differences.

arbitrageur
> One who engages in **arbitrage**.

articles of association

Document which must be filed with the **memorandum of association** when a company is formed. The articles are effectively the contractual terms between shareholders and directors.

asset

Something of monetary value to a company, e.g. cash, debts, stock and property. Assets can be classified as **current** or **fixed**, or as **tangible** or **intangible**. (There are also other less common terms.) The opposite to an asset is a **liability**. Assets minus liabilities gives **net assets**.

asset backed

Applies to an investment whose value is represented by assets such as land or stocks, rather than an investment whose return is determined institutionally.

asset stripping

The practice of buying a company, not for its trading value, but for the value of the assets it owns. The asset stripper then sells the assets for a quick profit leaving him with a **shell company**.

associate member

Individual who is a member of the Stock Exchange but who is not a partner or director of a firm which is a member.

at best

Term used in giving instructions for stock to be bought or sold at the best possible price.

auditors

Accountants engaged by the shareholders to report whether the accounts are true and fair and comply with the Companies Act.

authorised capital

The maximum amount of capital which a company's **memorandum of association** allows it to issue.

averaging

The practice of buying more shares when their value falls so as to reduce the impact of short-term fluctuations.

back-in
> Defence to a takeover, similar to a **poison pill** whereby shareholders can sell their shares back to the company.

back-to-back loan
> A loan in one country or currency which is backed by a loan in another country or currency to provide security against currency fluctuations.

backwardation
> Where, in the **futures** market, the price for a future delivery is less than the cash price or spot price.

balance sheet
> One of the two main accounting statements (the other is the **profit and loss account**) published at least annually by all companies. It lists all values of **assets** and **liabilities** as at a certain date (usually the financial year-end or the end of a quarter of such a year) and shows how this is represented by **share capital**, **retained profit**, etc.

ballot
> A means of allocating shares on a random basis when an issue is oversubscribed.

Baltic Exchange
> The London-based exchange where shippers and shipbrokers ply for cargo.

bargain
> A purchase or sale on the Stock Exchange.

base rate
> The rate, expressed as a percentage, decided by the banks from which most other rates used in lending are calculated.

basis point
> The unit of an index. If an index increases from 300 to 306, it has increased by six basis points which, in this example, is equivalent to 2 per cent.

bear

Someone who believes that share prices will fall. The opposite is a **bull**.

bear hug

An indication to the board of a **target company** that an offer is under consideration. See also **strong bear hug** and **teddy bear hug**.

bearer stock

A stock which has no registered owner, but is owned by whoever holds the certificate itself. Dividends are usually claimed by using **coupons**. These are fairly rare because of the inherent security problem.

bed and breakfast

The practice of selling an investment (or any other type of asset) very soon after buying it, either to realise a **capital gain** or to reduce the liability of capital gains tax by using the annual exemption.

benchmark

Notable achievement by a company expected to lead to an increase in its share price.

beneficial owner

The person entitled to the ultimate rights of an investment (or other property). A person who is the **registered owner** but not the beneficial owner is a **nominee**.

beta factor

The factor used to measure the movement of a *particular* share, or class of shares, independently from the movement of shares generally (measured by the **alpha coefficient**).

beta share

A share with a full listing but which is not traded enough to be an **alpha share**.

bid

Attempt at a **takeover**.

bid/offer spread

The difference between the buying and selling price.

This difference is the **turn** or profit to the market-maker (or equivalent). It is in addition to his **commission**.

bid price

The price at which a market-maker (or equivalent) will buy back stock.

bid valuation

Where unit trust managers value bids and offers according to the actual sale cost of holdings within the fund. The usual practice within a unit trust is to match buyers and sellers. Bid valuation is needed when sales exceed purchases.

Big Bang

The package of Stock Exchange reforms introduced in the UK on 27 October 1986. The reforms were designed to meet the independent objectives of making London part of a worldwide exchange (with New York and Tokyo); to remove old restrictive practices and to modernise operations by using computerised equipment.

black book

A preplanned defence to a **takeover bid**.

blue button

Trainee market-maker, allowed to collect prices but not to transact bargains.

blue chip

A company or investment perceived as solid and reliable. Such a company will often be a well-established large company which is a household name and has enjoyed consistent growth.

blue chip out

Where a company does not seek a **quotation** of its own but is bought out by a **blue chip** company.

boiler room

High pressure sales techniques used to sell shares of doubtful worth. The term first arose in the Netherlands in 1986.

bond

Fixed interest security. Bonds are particularly popular with the Government.

bondwashing

The practice of selling a bond **cum dividend** so that the accrued dividend is taxed as a capital gain rather than as income. The tax laws were changed in 1985 to render bondwashing ineffective.

bonus issue

An issue of shares to existing shareholders in ratio to their existing holdings. It is usually either a means of capitalising retained profit or of splitting high valued shares into lower valued units. A bonus issue is also known as a **scrip issue**.

bonus share

Share issued in a **bonus issue**.

book

Investments held to the account of a broker or investment manager for resale.

boot strap

A cash offer for a **controlling interest** followed by a lower offer for the rest of the target company's shares.

bought deal

A transaction which is done for a fixed fee rather than for **turn** or **commission**.

boutique

Financial service business operated from shop premises.

box

Another name for a **book**.

break-forward

A forward contract in the international money market which can be unwound at a predetermined rate. The holder can thus benefit from a currency movement in his favour, but sells some of the upside advantage to restrict his risk to the predetermined rate.

bridge financing

Short-term funding, usually to cover a short period while long-term funding is being organised.

broad money

The colloquial description of **M3**.

bubble

Company whose high share price is due to **hype** rather than any intrinsic worth.

bucket shop

Broker who is not a member of a recognised stock exchange.

buffer

Unused credit or cash facilities.

bull

Someone who believes share prices will rise. If it is generally expected that share prices will rise, the market is said to be bullish. The opposite to a bull is a **bear**.

bulldog

A security denominated in sterling but not issued by the UK government.

bullet

Fixed interest security with only one maturity date.

burn-out turnaround

Restructuring of a company which would otherwise go into liquidation.

burn rate

Rate at which a new venture uses up its **venture capital**.

Business Expansion Scheme

A scheme whereby generous tax incentives are given to those who invest in private companies. The rules are complex, and the scheme is subject to many restrictions.

cd

Abbreviation of **cum dividend**.

call

1 Instalment in paying for shares when issued (or, more strictly, the request to pay the instalment). When all the calls have been paid, the shares are described as **fully paid up**.
2 Period in which trading is conducted on a particular market. It is led by a **call chairman** who invites bids and offers. Calls are usually held at the beginning or end of a trading session.

call option
> Right given to a market maker to buy a fixed number of shares at a specific price within a predetermined period.

cap
> Option to protect an investor from interest rates moving against him.

capital
> The total amount a company has to fund its operations. It includes **share capital**, **retained profit**, **reserves**, and, possibly loans such as preference shares and **debentures**.
>
> The word 'capital' has many other applications in distinguishing amounts from income or expenditure.

capital gains tax
> Tax payable on the profit of a capital gain which is not subject to income tax.

capital transfer tax
> Tax payable on gifts and inheritances. Since 1986 it has been known as **inheritance tax** and is only charged on transfers made on the transferor's death or in the previous seven years.

capitalisation
> The process of turning liquid funds into capital. It usually arises when **retained profit** is converted to shares by a **capitalisation** issue.

capitalisation issue
> **Bonus issue** which converts retained profit to share capital.

captive fund
> **Venture capital** fund wholly owned by a larger body.

car
> Another name for a **futures** contract.

carrot equity
> **Option** for managers or investors to **participate** in a company if it meets certain criteria.

carrying
> Lending or borrowing when trading futures.

cash and new

The deferment of settlement when stock is sold in one account and bought back in another. Broking commission is not payable.

cash cow

Profitable business used to fund other enterprises.

cash positive

The state when a company's trade is producing a profit.

cash settlement

Term used to describe deals where payment is required immediately and not be charged to an account.

cat

Discounted **zero coupon bond**.

certificate

The document evidencing ownership of stock. A certificate is only *conclusive* evidence for **bearer stock**.

certification

Marking the transfer deed by the Stock Exchange or Company's Registrar's when some, but not all, the stock is transferred.

channel

Charting term denoting the parallel lines between which a share price bounces.

chartist

Someone who predicts share movements by plotting them on a chart.

Chinese wall

Any arrangement whereby information known to one part of a business is deliberately not made known to another so as to prevent a conflict of interest, such as **insider trading**.

City

'The City' is the City of London and adjoining areas where financial transactions traditionally are made. Computer technology has made physical location less important.

City code

The usual term for the City Code on Takeovers and Mergers. It sets out the conduct which the Council for the Securities Industry expects to be followed by companies involved in a takeover or merger.

class

All shares, options or other type of security subject to the same rights.

client account

Bank account held by someone who trades for clients and containing only money belonging to those clients.

close

1 (noun) Closing period of a session.
2 (verb) Transact to clear an existing position.

close company

Company controlled by five or fewer people. Such companies have certain tax restrictions.

closing price

Last quoted prices at the end of a trading session.

closing sale

Sale of securities to close a long position.

collar

Combination of a **cap** and a floor forming a **straddle**, i.e. a combination of interest rates to protect against interest rate fluctuations.

commercial rate of interest

Rate of interest at which a commercial venture is worthwhile. It is the benchmark for many investment decisions, and is usually 2 or 3 per cent above the **base rate**.

commission

Payment on a pro-rata basis for services rendered.

commodities

Basic materials for which the market functions more efficiently if sold through a central house. Cereals, metals and rubber are commodities.

common stock
US term for **ordinary** share.

Companies House
Office of the DTI at which all companies are registered and to which annual returns must be submitted.

company doctor
Specialist in dealing with 'unhealthy' companies.

company secretary
Employee of the company entrusted with making sure that the company honours its legal obligations.

concert party
Secret arrangement whereby apparently unconnected shareholders are actually working together.

confirmation
When a share price moves in line with an appropriate index.

consideration
What is given by each party to the other in a contract. For a purchase or sale of shares, the considerations are usually shares and cash.

consolidated accounts
The accounts of a **group** reported as if the group were one entity.

Consols
Consolidated stock issued by the Government. They were first issued in the eighteenth century and carry interest at 2½ per cent. The price fluctuates in line with interest rates and is regarded as a guide to gilt-edged interest rates.

consumer capitalism
Conservative Government's policy of encouraging its citizens to buy shares.

contango
1 Carrying over the settlement of a transaction from one account to the next.
2 Difference between spot price and price paid for forward delivery.

Continuation Day
First day of a Stock Exchange account.

contract note
Written confirmation of a transaction in securities.

contract stamp duty
Fixed duty of a nominal amount paid on share dealing.

contrarian
Someone who swims against the general economic tide.

controlling interest
When a shareholder holds sufficient shares to be able to control the company. Any holding greater than 50 per cent is always a controlling interest, but where there are many shareholders holdings as low as 20 per cent can be a controlling interest.

convertible
Refers to loan stock which can be converted to equity capital.

corporate venturing
Investment by a large company in smaller companies.

corporation tax
Tax payable by a company on its profits.

council
Will usually refer to the Council of the Stock Exchange, its executive committee.

coupon
Detachable part of a share certificate or similar document against which a dividend is paid.

creeping takeover
Takeover achieved by slowly acquiring shares on the open market.

crown jewels
The company in a target group which the bidder is after. A defence to a hostile takeover is to sell the crown jewels only.

cum div or cum dividend
Refers to a share price which includes the right to a recently declared dividend.

cum pref
Abbreviation of **cumulative preference shares.**

cum rights
Refers to a share issue which includes the rights given in a recent rights issue.

cumulative preference share
Preference share where any unpaid interest from one year is automatically added to later years and not lost.

current asset
Asset other than a fixed asset. Current assets are cash, bank balances, short-term investments, debtors, prepayments and trading stock. Current assets minus liabilities is **working capital**.

current cost accounting
Method which adjusts the accounts to show the effects of inflation. No system has achieved general support. The requirement to prepare current cost accounts was withdrawn on 6 June 1985.

current liability
An amount which the company has to pay within one year.

current yield
Interest or dividend expressed as a percentage of its current market price.

cycle
Period in which a share price moves from a major low to a major high (or vice versa) and back again.

DTI
Abbreviation of 'Department of Trade and Industry', the Government department responsible for supervising companies. The department has the right to send in inspectors if it believes that company law has been broken.

dawn raid
When one company buys many shares in a target company before the market becomes aware of what is happening.

day order
 Order given to a broker which is valid for one day only.

dead cat bounce
 Temporary market recovery after a sustained decline.

death valley curve
 Period in which a new business is using up its venture capital before supporting itself from its own cashflow.

debenture
 Security, usually at a fixed interest rate, issued by a company and secured on its assets.

deep discount bond
 Bond issued at much less than its redemption value on a fixed date. The interest rate is low to maximise the element of capital gain.

deferred shares
 Ordinary shares whose right to a dividend ranks after other ordinary shares.

delivery
 Formal transfer of share certificate.

delta
 Factor by which an option price varies relative to the price of a convertible investment.

development capital
 Funds for an existing profitable business to expand.

dilute
 Reduce the voting power of a shareholding by increasing the number of shares or their voting power. The term is commonly used in connection with convertible loan stock.

discount
 Usually used to indicate that a security's price has been reduced to reflect the effects of a future event.

discounting
 Reduction in the market price of a security to increase its marketability.

dividend
>   Payment out of profits to a shareholder in the ratio of his shareholding.

dividend cover
>   Net earnings divided by net dividend.

dividend warrant
>   Cheque for the dividend with accompanying voucher.

double bottom
>   Charting method which assumes that once a share price has hit the same low twice, it will increase in value.

double option
>   **Traded option**, purchased for a premium, to declare oneself by a fixed date as either the buyer or seller.

double top
>   Charting method which assumes that once a share price has hit the same high twice, it will decrease in value.

Dow–Jones index
>   Index of the New York Stock Exchange.

down and dirty
>   Practice whereby major investors refinance a troubled company so that the minor shareholders' stakes would be diluted if they did not participate. This practice will usually be against UK company law.

drip-feed
>   Supply **venture capital** in stages.

drop-dead fee
>   Fee paid by bidders to lenders when an acquisition fails and the means of credit set up to finance the bid are not used.

drop-lock
>   Arrangement which allows a variable rate loan to become a fixed rate loan.

dual capacity
>   The arrangement whereby the **Big Bang** allows a stockbroker to be a market-maker.

dull

Indicates that prices are falling.

EB

Abbreviation of **early bargain**.

early bargain

Bargain agreed after the Stock Exchange has officially closed. Such a bargain is treated as having been done at the beginning of the next trading day.

earn-out

Arrangement by which managers can 'earn' shares.

earnings per share

Net profit after tax divided by the number of ordinary shares in issue.

earnings yield

Ratio of earnings to market capitalisation.

easier

Describes prices which are falling.

elves

Market analysts whose analysis is believed actually to control the workings of the market, particularly in Wall Street.

eps

Abbreviation of 'earnings per share'.

equities

Shares in companies as opposed to other types of investment such as gilts or property.

equity

The value of a company after all claims except the shareholders' have been met.

equity capital

Shareholders' capital

ethical investment

Investment motivated partly by non-financial factors, such as whether the company trades in South Africa, and whether it deals in arms, tobacco, etc.

Eurobond
>International bond issued outside the investor's own country

European monetary system
>System in which all EEC currencies, except sterling, are linked by preset exchange rates. Colloquially known as 'the snake'.

Eurosclerosis
>Sluggishness in the economies of European countries which prevents their participating in a world expansion.

evergreen fund
>Venture capital fund which lends money in stages rather than in one go.

ex div
>Abbreviation of 'ex dividend'.

ex dividend
>Without a dividend. Marked by a share price, it means that the purchaser of the share is not entitled to the next dividend.

ex growth
>A share which the Stock Exchange thinks will neither increase nor decrease in value.

ex-new
>A share whose price does not entitle the purchaser to take up an offer for new shares.

Exchequer stock
>A government security issued to meet a long-term liability.

exempt gilts
>Gilt which is paid gross, i.e. without deduction of income tax.

exercise notice
>Formal notice that an option holder is buying at the exercise price.

exercise price
>Price at which the buyer of a call option may buy the security.

exit
>   When a venture capitalist ends his relationship with the
>   company, usually by a flotation.

expiry date
>   Last date on which an option may be exercised.

exploding poison pills
>   Elaborate defence to a takeover. It basically involves
>   granting rights to preference shareholders which
>   'explode' on a takeover making the company too
>   expensive to acquire.

extraordinary general meeting
>   General meeting other than the **annual general meeting**.

extraordinary items
>   Items which contribute to a company's profit or loss but
>   which are outside its normal activities. Such items are
>   shown separately in the profit and loss account and are
>   not included in pre-tax profit and earnings per share.

FIMBRA
>   Abbreviation of Financial Intermediaries, Managers and
>   Brokers Regulatory Association, the body which
>   regulates the activities of those who market securities
>   and unit trusts to the public.

FT
>   Abbreviation of *The Financial Times*.

face value
>   Another term for 'par value' or 'nominal value'.

fat cat
>   Venture capitalist whose reward is excessive relative to
>   his investment.

final dividend
>   Dividend paid against the year-end results.

finance house
>   A company whose business is to lend money.

firm
>   Indicates that prices are rising.

fixed assets
Assets which a company uses (but does not consume) in the course of its business. It includes land, building, property, plant and machinery, furniture, etc.

fixed deposit
Money lent for a fixed period in which it cannot be withdrawn. It usually commands a higher interest rate than withdrawable funds.

fixed duty
Stamp duty at a fixed rate, i.e. not *ad valorem* **duty**.

fixed interest stock
A security which pays a fixed interest irrespective of the profit of whoever issued it. Local authorities and the Government issue such stock.

flag
1 Chartist term for a short-term reverse in a fast-moving upward or downward trend in share prices, taken to indicate a further move in the general trend.
2 Notification to a venture capitalist that something is wrong.

flat
Indicates that prices are falling.

flat yield
Where the **yield** neither increases nor decreases.

flip-in
Defence to a takeover in which existing shareholders have the right to buy further shares cheaply (usually at half price).

floating rate note
Loan stock whose interest rate floats with market interest rates.

floor
1 Interest rate option to protect the investor from interest rates falling below an agreed level (the 'floor'),
2 The trading floor of the Stock Exchange.

flotation
Issuing shares to the public for the first time.

Footsie

Nickname for Financial Times–Stock Exchange 100 share index. So called because of its abbreviation 'FT-SE 100'.

forward dealing

Striking a deal to buy or sell a holding in the future at a fixed price as a hedge against adverse movements in its value.

founder's share

Ordinary share held by the founder of a business. It often has deferred rights, ranking after other ordinary shares.

franked income

Investment income paid from a company's profits which have already borne corporation tax.

free issue

Another name for a **capitalisation issue**.

freeze-out

Pressure on minority shareholders to sell their holdings to a new owner.

friendly takeover

Takeover supported by the company being taken over.

fringe benefit

Any indirect benefit or 'perk'. For shareholders this means free or subsidised supply of the company's products or services.

front end load

Arrangement whereby the initial costs of a unit trust are charged early in the scheme with the result that less of the investor's money is invested.

fully paid

Shares where all the par value has been paid to the company. The opposite to partly paid.

fund manager

Person employed to manage an investment fund, sometimes according to fixed objectives (e.g. maximise capital growth).

futures
> Contracts to buy a **commodity** at a future date, as opposed to actuals.

gamma shares
> Shares mainly quoted on the USM.

gearing
> The ratio of share capital to borrowing. A company with high borrowings is highly geared. The investors of such a company will do better when the profits are high, and worse when profits are low.

general meeting
> Meeting of a company attended by shareholders. It will either be an **annual general meeting** or an **extraordinary general meeting**.

general undertaking
> Undertaking given by directors of a company seeking a USM listing that it will comply with the USM rules.

gilt-edged securities
> Another name for 'gilts'.

gilts
> Government securities.

GmbH
> Abbreviation of '*Gesellschaft mit beschränkter Haftung*', German for limited company.

go-go
> Fast growing (investment).

go nap
> Invest all one's assets in one enterprise. Alternatively make a firm commitment to a heavy investment.

Godfather offer
> A takeover offer that the target company cannot refuse.

going public
> Converting from a private company to a public company, by floating shares.

gold

The precious metal which traditionally provided the means for measuring all other monetary values (an arrangement known as the gold standard). The gold standard was replaced by the gold bullion standard in 1925 and the arrangement generally abolished in 1931. Gold, however, remains as both a source of investments and a general economic measurement, and is still used to settle international debts.

golden handcuffs

Financial arrangement to prevent staff leaving.

golden handshake

Payment to a retiring or leaving staff member.

golden hello

Financial inducement to recruit staff.

golden parachute

Clause in an employment contract which gives a director or senior employee a generous payment if his services are dispensed with. It is a device often used to counter takeover bids.

golden share

Strategic holding, usually by a government in an important industry to prevent another country from acquiring too much of it.

good-till-cancelled

An instruction which stands until cancelled.

Government securities

Securities issued by the Government. Also known as gilts.

Green book

The book giving the conditions for entry to the USM.

greenfield

Brand new venture.

greenmail

Payment made by a target company to a takeover bidder to prevent the takeover. It is usually made at a premium not available to other shareholders.

grey knight
 A counterbidder whose intentions are unclear, and is therefore a mixture of white knight and black knight.

grey market
 A market in shares which have not yet been issued.

grey wave
 Investment area with potential that may take more than the investor's lifetime to realise.

growth
 Increase in intrinsic value.

growth stock
 A security which shows continuous growth.

guaranteed income bond
 Investment instrument which offers fixed income and a guaranteed repayment of the investment at the end of a specified term. They are often issued by insurance companies.

hammered
 The process whereby a Stock Exchange member is regarded as unable to meet his or its debts. It is signalled by three bangs on the waiter's table. Unpaid debts are met from the Stock Exchange Compensation Fund.

hands off
 Investment policy whereby the investor refrains from exerting influence over the management even though he had the right to do so.

Hang Seng index
 Index of the Hong Kong stock exchange.

hard
 Indicates that prices are rising.

head and shoulders
 A chart pattern which looks a little like a picture of head and shoulders.

hedge
 Any arrangement whereby protection is afforded against adverse future conditions.

hemline theory
Theory that share prices rise in line with ladies' skirts.

historical cost accounts
Traditional accounts which ignore the effects of inflation.

holding company
A company which (usually) does not trade itself but owns shares in companies that do.

hostile takeover
A takeover resisted by the target company.

hype
Marketing of securities on bases other than intrinsic worth.

IPO
Abbreviation of **Initial Public Offering**.

impact day
The day on which flotation terms are first made public.

in-the-money option
A call option where the exercise price is below the current market price.

income bond
Another name for a guaranteed income bond.

index fund
Fund designed to move in line with stock values generally.

index-linked
Related to an index, usually the retail price index. Index-linked gilts were first issued in 1981. Their value is linked to the RPI and thereby provides a hedge against inflation.

indicator
Price investigation designed to investigate the reason for a price move.

inflation
Increase in the price of goods and services. It is usually expressed as the percentage by which the Retail Price Index increases the RPI for one year previously.

inheritance tax
New name for capital transfer tax from 1986, reflecting the fact that tax is not always payable on lifetime gifts.

initial public offering
US term for **flotation**.

innoventure
US colloquialism for an innovative venture.

insider dealing
A process by which a person in a privileged position of knowledge regarding a company may use that knowledge for his own purposes by buying or selling shares. It has been illegal since 1980, and has been more effectively monitored from 1986 by an agreement with the US Securities Exchange Commission and by the Financial Services Act 1986.

intellectual property
Assets such as patents, copyright and know-how.

interim dividend
Dividend paid during the year, as opposed to **final dividend**.

intrapreneur
An employee who otherwise acts like an entrepreneur.

intrinsic value
Build-up in an investment's value, not necessarily reflected in its price.

investment
Temporarily ceding the use of one's money with a view to receiving a larger sum.

investment bond
Single premium life insurance policy funded by asset-backed investment.

investment club
Group of investors who pool their funds for collective investment.

investment company
A company whose business is investing.

investment income surcharge
> Additional income tax paid on large enough investment earnings. It was abolished in 1984 though an equivalent remains for some trusts.

investment trust
> A company which uses its capital to invest in other companies, and issues marketable shares for that purpose.

issued capital
> The amount of **authorised capital** which a company has issued.

issuing house
> Financial institution which deals with the issuing of shares.

jobber
> A dealer on the Stock Exchange. Known as **market-makers** since the Big Bang.

joint investment
> Investment made by more than one person.

Jonestown defence
> A measure to counter a takeover bid which is so extreme as to be regarded as suicidal.

junk bond
> Loan stock based on an overvalued security. Often used in takeover manoeuvres.

kerb trading
> Trading after the market has closed for the day. Now usually only applied to the metals market.

key reversal
> Chart term denoting a new peak or trough which is not sustained, usually as a result of a change in the company's fortunes.

kiss/kiss principle
> The principle that people will only invest in ideas they can understand. The term is supposedly derived as an acronym of 'Keep It Simple, Stupid'.

LIBOR

Abbreviation of **London Inter-Bank Offered Rate**.

LIFFE

Abbreviation of **London International Financial Futures Exchange**. The abbreviation is pronounced 'liffy'.

Lady Macbeth strategy

Takeover strategy where what appears to be a **white knight** suddenly changes sides.

laundering

Process of passing money through different channels either to make it hard to trace (e.g. for tax evasion) or to avoid some inconvenient regulation (such as exchange controls).

lead investor

Largest investor (possibly a venture capitalist) who becomes involved in the management on behalf of other investors.

leaseback

When a company sells an asset and then leases it back, thus converting an asset to cash but incurring a current liability.

lemon

Investment which is bad because it 'ripens' too soon. The opposite is a **plum**.

letter of allotment

Notification of how many shares an investor has been allocated in an issue.

letter of indemnity

Letter sent when a share certificate has been lost. It indemnifies the company against any claim arising from the original certificate.

letter of renunciation

Exercise of a right to sell shares allocated in a rights issue.

leverage

American term for **gearing**.

leveraged buyout
When a small company with limited assets borrows heavily to take over a larger target company.

limit order
Order to a broker placing financial limits outside which shares may not be bought or sold.

limited company
A registered company which enjoys **limited liability**.

limited liability
When liability to third parties is limited to a predetermined amount. For limited companies the limit is the company's own resources. Unlike a partnership, the members themselves are protected.

liquid assets
Assets which are consumed in the course of the business, and have a life of less than one year. It comprises cash, debts, prepayments and stock.

liquidation
The process by which a company is removed from the control of its directors (to a liquidator) with a view to its being **wound up**.

listed company
Company quoted on the Stock Exchange.

listing
Becoming quoted on the London Stock Exchange.

listing agreement
The agreement by directors on listing to observe Stock Exchange rules.

living dead
Company which is just about trading profitably.

Lloyds
Corporation in London which provides the main insurance market.

loan stock
Security by which investors lend money to the company at a fixed interest rate. The commonest form is the **debenture**.

lock up
Agreement between bidder and target company designed to exclude new bidders.

London Inter-bank Offering Rate
Rate at which London banks lend money to each other. Usually known as LIBOR.

London International Financial Futures Exchange
Market for **futures**. Commonly known as LIFFE.

long
An investment which is expected to take some time to realise its potential.

long form report
A report prepared by an accountant which provides information on a company to an issuing house before flotation of the company.

long-term gilt
Government security repayable in 10 to 15 years' time.

longs
Long-term gilts.

M0, etc.
Measurements of the money supply. M0 measures coins and bank notes, and banks' balances with the Bank of England. Higher numbers add other figures up to M3 which effectively includes all bank balances.

MLR
Abbreviation of **minimum lending rate**.

MMC
Abbreviation of **Monopolies and Mergers Commission**.

managed portfolio
A **portfolio** in which the decisions to buy and sell are made other than by the shares' owner.

management buyout
Purchase of a company by those who already run it.

market order
Order to sell a security immediately at market price.

market price
The price for which a security (or anything else) can actually be sold.

marking up
Increasing the price of a security because of expected demand rather than because of any increase in the security's intrinsic value.

marzipan layer
The layer of senior management immediately below directors and senior partners, i.e. just below the 'icing'. They have a much lower profile than the top men even though they can often exert as much or even more influence.

matched bargain
Transaction in which a sale is directly related to a purchase.

maximum slippage
The maximum amount by which a company can use its venture capital before being regarded as insolvent.

medium-term gilt
Government security repayable in 5 to 10 years' time.

mediums
Medium-term gilts.

megabid
Very large takeover bid.

meltdown
Economic collapse in a particular sector.

memorandum of association
Document which must be filed when a company is formed. It is effectively the company's constitution.

merchant bank
Financial institution offering various services, including those of an issuing house.

mezzanine finance
Venture capital to an established business in a hybrid form between equity and debt.

middle price
: Security price which is the average of the buying and selling price, i.e. halfway between the **spread**.

milestone
: Important achievement by a company expected to increase the share price.

minimum lending rate
: The rate at which the Bank of England lends to the money market. It is used as a basis for setting most interest rates (e.g. MLR + 3 per cent).

minimum offering period
: The shortest time that a tender offer stays open.

minority interest
: Shareholdings other than a **controlling interest**.

modern portfolio theory
: The theory that share prices move according to the alpha and beta factors.

momentum
: Speed at which a share price rises or falls.

money market
: Market for short-term loans, usually in bills of exchange, trade bills and Treasury bills.

money supply
: Measure of the amount of money in the national economy. See **M0, etc.**

Monopolies and Mergers Commission
: Statutory body whch regulates takeovers which result in the new combine having a monopoly (i.e. more than 25 per cent of the market).

mortgage debenture
: Loan stock secured on particular assets.

moving average
: A means of detecting general trends from short-term trends by taking the average for a period.

mutual funds
: US term for **unit trust**.

NASDIM
>Abbreviation of **National Association of Security Dealers and Investment Managers.**

NL
>Abbreviation of 'no liability', Australian equivalent to **plc**.

NPV
>Abbreviation of **no par value**.

NV
>Abbreviation of '*Naamloze Venootschap*', a Dutch stock corporation (roughly equivalent to a public company).

narrow money
>Another name for the **M0** measure of money supply.

National Savings
>Simple deposit account arrangement using post offices. It was formed in 1969 and was previously known as Post Office Savings Department.

near money
>Investments which are **liquid** enough to be regarded as the equivalent of cash.

net assets
>The value of a company's assets less its liabilities.

net current assets
>The value of a company's current assets less its current liabilities.

net profit
>A company's profit after deducting all expenses, including all interest payments. The figure usually quoted is before deduction of tax, ordinary share dividends and **extraordinary items**.

new issue
>Share floated on the Stock Exchange for the first time.

new time
>The arrangement whereby bargains struck on the last two days of an **account** may be regarded as having been done in the next account.

Nikkei–Dow index
Japanese equivalent to the Financial Times ordinary share index.

nil paid
Shares on which no money has yet been paid. It usually applies to a rights issue.

no par value
A share without a par value, illegal in the UK, but common in the US, Australia and New Zealand.

nominal price
Equivalent to a traded price when such is not readily available.

nominal value
Par value of a share.

nominee
Person who holds shares for the **beneficial interest** of someone else.

OTC
Abbreviation of **Over the Counter**.

OY
Abbreviation of '*Osakeyhito*', a Finnish limited company.

offer for sale
Offer to the public of shares.

offer price
Price at which shares are offered. The alternative is a **striking price**.

Official List
Daily list prepared by the Stock Exchange recording details of bargains.

offshore funds
Fund similar to a **unit trust** but operated from outside the jurisdiction of the DTI and the UK tax authorities.

option
The right to do something (usually buy or sell).

ordinary share
> Part ownership of a limited company, usually with voting rights, as opposed to preference shares, etc.

out of the money
> Traded option term meaning that the **exercise price** is above the security's market price.

Over the Counter
> Market for securities outside the control of the Stock Exchange.

Overbought
> Refers to a company or a market when it is believed that **profit taking** is overdue.

oversold
> Refers to a market which is believed to have declined too quickly, i.e. to have over-reacted.

oversubscribed
> When subscriptions exceed shares available for allotment.

P/E
> Abbreviation of **price/earnings ratio**.

PEP
> Abbreviation of **Personal Equity Plan**.

plc
> Suffix to a company's name denoting that it is a **public limited company**.

PSBR
> Abbreviation of **Public Sector Borrowing Requirement**.

Pac-man defence
> Defence to a takeover in which the target company bids for its bidder.

par value
> The face value of a share, often 25p. Also known as the **nominal value**.

pari passu
> Latin for 'equal in its position'. It is used to describe shares which are being issued with the same status as existing shares.

participate
>Share in the profits, as opposed to receiving a fixed rate of interest.

partly paid
>Refers to a share whose par value has not been fully paid.

passive management
>Portfolio management which does not buy or sell shares, believing that the portfolio is constructed well enough to withstand share price movements.

pearl
>Profitable investment which compensates for unprofitable ones.

penny share
>A share available at very low cost. Such shares can have great investment potential.

personal equity plan
>Managed portfolio which, from 1 January 1987, offers generous tax incentives for private investment.

pink form
>Preferential share application, usually restricted to 10 per cent of an issue.

placing
>Process by which a stockbroker/issuing house/sponsor allots shares among his clients and elsewhere.

poison pills
>Defence to a takeover aimed to turn the target company into a liability should the bid succeed. A company ploy is to issue convertible securities.

popular capitalism
>Another name for **consumer capitalism**.

porcupine provisions
>Provisions built into a company's articles to prevent a takeover.

portfolio
>Collection of investments viewed as one entity.

preference shares
> Shares with a fixed dividend, and with prior claims to both dividends and capital repayment over ordinary shares.

pre-tax profit
> Net profit before tax (and ordinary share dividends and extraordinary items).

premium
> Excess of a share's market value over its par value.

price/earnings ratio
> The market price of a share divided by its annual dividend.

prime rate
> US equivalent to **base rate**.

private company
> Company whose shares are subject to restrictions on purchase.

privatisation
> Process by which state corporations are floated, the opposite to nationalisation.

probate price
> Share values as used in valuing a dead person's estate. It uses the **quarter-up** rule.

profit and loss account
> Financial statement of a company showing how much profit or loss has been earned in a fixed period.

prospectus
> Document issued in connection with an **offer for sale**. It is subject to strict legal provisions.

proxy
> Person voting on another's behalf.

public company
> A company whose shares may be freely bought and sold.

pullback
Chart term for a short-term move back toward a chart pattern against the underlying trend.

put option
Option to sell (as opposed to a **call option**).

put through
Special dealing procedure for very large quantities of shares.

quarter up
Share valuation method used in probate and for tax purposes. The shares are valued at the buying price plus a quarter of the difference between that and the selling price.

quotation
The buying and selling prices of a security as shown in the **Official List**.

quoted company
Company which appears on the **Official List**.

RPI
Abbreviation of **retail price index**.

raider
Initiator of a hostile takeover bid.

random walk theory
Theory that share prices follow no set pattern and that **charting** is therefore a waste of time.

reaction
A short-term reversal of a major trend.

recovery stock
Stock which has fallen in value but which is believed will return to its previous value.

redeemable
Refers to debentures and similar forms of loan stock which the company may redeem by buying back for cancellation.

redemption date
  Date when debentures may be redeemed.

register
  A list of names, usually one which has to be kept by law. A company must keep registers of its members (shareholders), directors, company secretaries, directors' interests, directors' shareholdings, etc.

registered owner
  Name of the shareholder as it appears in the register of members. The person may be the **beneficial owner** or a **nominee**.

relative strength
  Price performance of a share compared with other prices or an index-based ratio.

renunciation
  Selling or giving up the right to allotted shares (or units in a unit trust).

replacement capital
  Shares sold by an entrepreneur to a venture capitalist.

repurchase
  Purchase of a share by the company which originally issued it.

reserves
  Accumulated profit not distributed to shareholders.

resistance line
  Line on a chart below which a share price does not fall.

Retail Price Index
  A number calculated on the basis of prices of a representative sample of retail goods. The increase in the index from one year to the next is the popular measure of inflation.

retained profit
  That part of a company's profit which it keeps for further development and does not distribute as a dividend.

return on capital
  Ratio between earned profit and investment.

reverse takeover
When a private company takes over a public company.

reverse yield gap
Extra earnings that could have been made if, instead of investing the money, it had been placed on deposit.

rights issue
An issue of shares whereby existing shareholders are invited to subscribe at preferential terms in proportion to their existing holdings.

risk
Either the amount that can be lost in an investment, or the chance of losing it.

SA
Abbreviation of either *'Société Anonyme'*, a French, Belgian or Luxembourg limited company; or *'Sociedad Anonima'*, a Spanish limited company.

SARL
Abbreviation of *'Sociedad Anónima com Résponsabilidade Limitada'*, a Portuguese joint stock company (roughly equivalent to a public company).

SEAQ
Abbreviation of **Stock Exchange Automated Quotations System**.

SEC
Abbreviation of **Securities Exchange Commission**.

SIB
Abbreviation of **Securities and Investments Board**.

SRO
Abbreviation of **self-regulatory organisation**.

sale and leaseback
A means by which a company with a liquidity problem obtains working capital by selling a fixed asset to a lessor and then leases the asset.

sandbag
Defence to a takeover in which the target company pretends to be interested but is actually protracting discussions in the hopes that a **white knight** will turn up.

scorched earth

Defence to a takeover by damaging the company's financial position to make it unattractive to the bidder. This usually involves borrowing money at exorbitant rates. It is often a suicidal policy.

scrip

Share certificates and similar documents.

scrip issue

Another name for a **bonus issue**.

second round financing

Additional capital sought by companies to finance products already launched.

sector

Classification of types of security, e.g. 'financial sector'.

Securities and Investments Board

Main regulatory body set up to supervise implementation of the Financial Services Act 1986.

Securities Exchange Commission

US body set up in 1934 which monitors US share dealings.

security

Any saleable document or right connected with finance. It includes shares, gilts, debentures, units in a unit trust, options, and rights to borrow and lend money. It excludes insurance policies.

seed capital

Money provided to fund a new business or a new venture by an existing company.

Self-Regulatory Organisation

An organisation which regulates its members in accordance with the Financial Services Act 1986. The Stock Exchange is such a body.

self-tender

Offer by tender by a company for its own shares.

Sepon

Acronym of Stock Exchange Pool Nominees, which is the official nominee company whch holds all stock sold during the course of settlement.

settlement date

Date on which a contract must be paid.

sexy

Describes a share regarded as having good investment potential.

SIB

Abbreviation for **Securities and Investments Board**.

share

Part ownership of a limited company. See **'A' shares**, **deferred shares**, **founders' shares**, **ordinary shares**, and **preference shares**.

share option

Traded option in an equity share.

shareholder

Owner of **shares**.

shell company

Company which has ceased active trading, but is kept alive for other purposes.

short covering

The **bear** tactic of selling a security in the hope of buying it at a cheaper price.

short form report

Accountant's report included in a **prospectus** dealing with the company's track record.

short-term gilt

Government security repayable in five years or less.

shorts

Short-term gilts.

show stopper

Defence to a takeover bid by a target company issuing a lawsuit against the bidder alleging some defect in the bidder's offer.

silver wheelchair

Another (less popular) name for **golden parachute**.

single capacity

The restriction whereby a stockbroker and stockjobber/market-maker may only act as such and not do the other's job.

sleeping economy

Investments, etc. with no apparent owner, usually because the original owner has died and the inheritors don't know of their existence.

slippage

Underperformance of a new capital.

slump

Point at which economic activity or values are at their lowest.

smokestack industries

Traditional manufacturing and engineering businesses.

snake

The **European Monetary System**.

social ownership

Labour party's alternative to **consumer capitalism**, involving state ownership and control of strategic industries. The differences between social ownership and nationalisation remain unclear.

soft

Indicates that prices are falling.

SpA

Abbreviation of '*Societá Per Azioni*', an Italian joint stock company, roughly equivalent to a public company.

special situation

An unusual factor which is likely to affect a share price. Examples include a new discovery and sale of a loss-making subsidiary.

speculator

Short-term investor.

split trust
> Unit trust in which the capital growth and income-earning functions are separated to meet differing needs of unitholders.

sponsor
> Person responsible for issuing the **prospectus**.

spot price
> Current cash price, usually for a commodity or foreign currency.

stag
> One who buys a new issue in the hope of immediately selling it for a profit.

stag-hunter
> Someone employed to sift applications for new issues to spot improper applications (usually from one person submitting more applications under different names).

staggered directorship
> Defence to a takeover in which directors' terms are staggered so that the bidder cannot control the board.

stamp duty
> Tax payable against the documents used for certain transactions.

standstill agreement
> Agreement between a bidder and target company that the bidder will buy no more shares in the target company.

star
> Investment that does so well it pays for others that don't many times over. It is more successful than a **plum**.

statement of adjustment
> Accountant's report which reconciles the **short-form report** with the **annual accounts**.

stock
> US term for shares. Also used in the UK either to mean shares collectively, or similar securities sold by value rather than number. Such stocks are usually sold in blocks of £100.

Stock Exchange
Place where shares and other securities may be bought and sold. When written with capital letters it refers to the stock exchange in London.

Stock Exchange Automated Quotations Service
Computerised share-dealing service used on the Stock Exchange.

stockbroker
Someone who buys and sells securities for clients. He often also provides related services, such as advice and accounting.

stockjobber
Another name for a **jobber**.

stop-loss
A system whereby shares are automatically sold when they fall to a certain figure, thus preventing further loss.

striking price
Price at which a security is sold under a sale by **tender**.

strong
Indicates that prices are rising.

strong bear hug
Public notice to a target company of an intended takeover.

stuffed
Colloquialism denoting that too many of one share are held.

sub-underwriting
When an underwriter underwrites another underwriter.

subsidiary
A company where more than 50 per cent of its equity capital is held by another company (known as the **holding company** or **parent company**).

sunrise industries
Industries in sectors which are gaining in popularity, e.g. electronics.

sunset industries
Industries in decline.

supermajority
Requirement that certain resolutions need majorities bigger than 50 per cent.

supply and demand
Price determining mechanism whereby prices rise and fall until supply matches demand.

support line
Line on a chart below which a share price does not fall.

switch
Transfer from one type of investment to another.

takeover
When one company acquires control of another by acquiring shares to make its holding more than 50 per cent.

Talisman
Acronym of Transfer Accounting Lodgement for Investors, Stock MANagement for market-makers. Stock Exchange computerised transfer system for most UK shares.

tandem companies
Companies with the same shareholders.

tangible asset
A fixed asset which has a physical existence (e.g. plant, buildings, cars) unlike intangible assets (goodwill, patents, know-how).

tap stock
Gilts which were undersubscribed at issue and have therefore been taken up by the Government Broker who gradually releases them on the market.

target company
Company for which another company is launching a takeover bid.

TAURUS

Acronym of Transfer and AUtomated Registration of Uncertified Stock. A Stock Exchange computer system which avoids the need for contract notes and which should be available in 1988 or 1989.

tax credit

Document showing the tax already paid on the accompanying dividend.

teddy bear hug

Indication from a **target company** that it will welcome a takeover but only at a higher price than currently offered.

ten times winner

Company which provides a tenfold return on investment.

tender

Subscription method whereby investors offer the price as well as stating how much security they want.

Third Market

The Stock Exchange's market for small companies which do not qualify for the USM or to be listed.

tiger

Treasury investment Growth Receipts, first launched in 1982. The investment is in US treasury bonds and all interest is rolled up.

TOPIC

Acronym of Teletext Output of Price Information by Computer. Screen-based price and information system used by Stock Exchange.

track record

Financial history of a company.

trade cycle

Period from boom to slump in a particular trade.

traded option

Option which has a value and therefore can itself be traded.

trading profit
Profit earned by a company from its normal activities, i.e. excluding such things as extraordinary items and investment income.

traditional option
Option to buy shares but so constructed that the option itself is not saleable.

tranche funding
Providing capital to a company on a piecemeal basis as certain criteria are met.

transfer
Process by which a shareholder passes ownership of his shares to another.

transfer deed
Document used to transfer shares.

transmit
Process by which shares change ownership other than by the voluntary act of the shareholder, e.g. on a shareholder's death.

Treasury
Government department entrusted with managing the economy.

Treasury bill
Bill of exchange issued weekly by the Government in large amounts to discount houses. They are repayable at three months.

Treasury stock
Collective name for all gilts.

trendline
Line on a chart indicating general movement of share prices.

triple witching hour
The last hour on the third Friday of March, June, September and December when, in Wall Street, contracts simultaneously expire on futures, options on indices and options on stocks. (The result is chaos.)

trust
> Body established to look after the interests of others.

turkey
> Dud investment.

turn
> Profit margin between the buying and selling prices.

USM
> Abbreviation of **Unlisted Securities Market**.

uncertificated
> Refers to units in a unit trust which are too small to justify the cost of issuing a new certificate. This usually arises when dividends are reinvested.

undated stock
> Fixed interest stock with no redemption date.

underwriting
> Guaranteeing (for a commission) to take up any unsubscribed shares.

unearned income
> Old name for **investment income**.

unfranked income
> Investment income on which income tax has not already been paid.

unit trust
> Managed share portfolio in which subscribers invest by buying units.

unlisted security
> Security not listed on the Stock Exchange but may be traded on the USM.

Unlisted Securities Market
> Market regulated by the Stock Exchange for trading in securities not listed on the Stock Exchange.

unsecured
> Not backed by any specific rights against specified assets.

valuation
> Estimate of a portfolio's worth.

value added tax
Sales tax charged on supplies of most goods and services, including most stockbrokers' commissions.

venture capital
Money provided as capital for a brand new business or activity.

virgin
Someone who has not dealt in a particular share before.

volume
Quantity of business done in a particular security.

voting rights
The rights of each class of shareholder to participate in the affairs of the company.

vulture capitalist
Venture capitalist who demands too much return on his investment.

Wall Street
New York stock exchange.

war loan
A gilt at 3½% interest with no redemption date, initially raised to fund the Second World War.

warehousing
The practice of buying up shares in collaboration with the company to force up the price.

warrant
Security issued by the Stock Exchange giving the holder the right to buy a specific share at a set price on a fixed date.

weighted ballot
Allocation of shares in an oversubscribed issue which is biased so that small investors get proportionately more of the number of shares for which they applied.

white knight
Welcome takeover bidder who thwarts an unwelcome one.

winding up
Process by which a company ceases to exist.

window
> An investment which allows the investor to have a close look at something, usually new technology.

withholding tax
> Tax deducted at source on overseas dividends.

within the account
> Refers to a sale and purchase of the same security within one **account**.

working capital
> Those current assets which can quickly be turned to cash (i.e. cash, bank balances, short-term investments, debtors, prepayments and trading stock).

xd
> Abbreviation for **ex dividend**.

yellow book
> The Stock Exchange's rules regarding listing. The proper title is *Admission of Securities to Listing*. The book is a loose-leaf work in a lurid binder.

yield
> The dividend payment calculated by reference to the share's market price.

yield gap
> Difference between the average yield on long-dated gilts and on shares.

zebra
> An investment similar to a **tiger** first issued in 1985 designed to be taxed heavily on an annual basis but providing good capital growth.

zero coupon bond
> Investment which offers no dividend (or equivalent) at all. It therefore is cheap to buy and provides good capital growth.

Index

Record of share transactions

Date	Details	No.	Bank	Capital	Dividend			Other

Record of share transactions

Date	Details	No.	Bank	Shares				Other

185

Record of share transactions

	Date	Details	No.	Bank	Capital	Dividend			Other

Record of share transactions

Date	Details	No.	Bank	Shares				Other

Record of share transactions

Date	Details	No.	Bank	Capital	Dividend			Other

Record of share transactions

Date	Details	No.	Bank	Shares			Other	

Record of share transactions

Date	Details	No.	Bank	Capital	Dividend			Other